Praise for
Miss Hildreth Wore Brown
Anecdotes of a Southern Belle

"Olivia deBelle Byrd follows in the footsteps of Southern humorists Fanny Flagg and Bailey White to create a delightful book of personal essays dedicated to delving into the mysteries of the modern Southern Belle—a woman no longer lost in coy mincing, but straight talking, cheap, and spunky enough to reject overpriced coffee and Victoria's Secret. With a dry wit worthy of Dorothy Parker, Byrd muses on everything from the state of our Christmas sweaters to the great assumption of Southern life—our mamas were crazy, so it isn't a great surprise we get a little sideways. *Miss Hildreth Wore Brown* is a great gift book, a great take-to-the-hospital book; possibly even a great take-to-the-viewing book to give the bereaved a laugh while they loll around the funeral home. A must-have for anyone with a taste for the absurd and a sweet tooth for all things Southern."

—JANIS OWENS,
author of *My Brother Michael*

"With *Miss Hildreth Wore Brown*, Olivia deBelle Byrd proves that she is the real thing—an authentic Southern Belle with stories galore. I can't wait to give this hilarious and heartwarming book to all my sweet friends."

—CASSANDRA KING,
author of *The Same Sweet Girls*

"As a fifth generation Southerner, I thought I knew all there was to know about Southern culture. However, Olivia deBelle Byrd has taught me a thing or two. *Miss Hildreth Wore Brown* covers everything from Sunday church, beauty pageants and Northern exposure with humorous insight. This is one that you'll want to savor with a mint julep!"

—MICHAEL MORRIS,
author of *A Place Called Wiregrass*

"Olivia deBelle Byrd is a wonderful writer if you happen to enjoy wit, talent, charm, and good looks. Anyone who has ever cracked a grin at the works of Nora Ephron or Fannie Flagg owes it to herself to read *Miss Hildreth Wore Brown*, which is the warmest, wisest, funniest book I've read in a month of Sundays. It's like lunch with your wittiest friends—full of heart, love, and juicy gossip. It contains so many hilarious lines I can't wait to dine out and pretend I was clever enough to come up with them myself!"

—ROBERT LELEUX,
author of *The Memoirs of a Beautiful Boy*

"I'm warning you, this book will knock you to the floor quicker than Holy Ghost wine—you won't know what hit 'cha, but you won't be able to stop laughing. (One more thing—but promise not to say nothing—I think it's pitiful the way Olivia carries on about her husband Tommy in the pages of this book. That poor man—I heard Tommy's so upset he's threatening to run off with Benny Hinn's ex-wife.)"

KAREN SPEARS ZACHARIAS,
author of *Will Jesus Buy Me a Double-Wide?*
('Cause I Need More Room for My Plasma TV)

"*Miss Hildreth Wore Brown* is the perfect guide to becoming a good Southerner for those not inclined to be nice. We have long known that a Southern woman can say anything about anyone and be excused if they finish it with: *Bless her heart*!"

—RON HART,
syndicated Southern humorist and author of
No Such Thing as a Pretty Good Alligator Wrestler

"Although my own deep Southern roots go back to more sharecroppers than characters like Olivia deBelle Byrd's Miss Hildreth (whom Huck Finn would have identified as one of "the Aristocracy"), I nodded often in recognition of my own experience and laughed out loud many times as I savored Byrd's down-home stories. Pour yourself a glass of iced tea, turn off your cell phone, and settle in for a delightful read."

—GLORIA PIPKIN,
great-granddaughter of a Civil War widow,
longtime former teacher, author, and editor

Miss Hildreth Wore Brown

Miss Hildreth Wore Brown

Anecdotes of a Southern Belle

Olivia deBelle Byrd

Olivia deBelle Byrd

New York

Miss Hildreth Wore Brown
Anecdotes of a Southern Belle

Like all good Southern stories, embellishments and exaggeration have been added to these real events.

Cover Design by: Rachel Lopez - Rachel@r2cdesign.com and Nancy Winkelmann

ISBN 978-1-60037-748-8

Library of Congress Control Number: 2010920116

Morgan James Publishing
1225 Franklin Ave., STE 325
Garden City, NY 11530-1693
Toll Free 800-485-4943
www.MorganJamesPublishing.com

In an effort to support local communities, raise awareness and funds, Morgan James Publishing donates one percent of all book sales for the life of each book to Habitat for Humanity. Get involved today, visit **www.HelpHabitatForHumanity.org**.

This book is dedicated to Linda, my muse, to Kendall and Pat, two of the greatest Southern ladies to ever grace my life, and to the joys of my life, my husband, Tommy, and my children, Tommy Jr. and Elizabeth.

Acknowledgments

This book would never have been published if not for two people. Michael Morris, a wonderful Southern author of *A Place Called Wiregrass* and *A Slow Way Home*, took a fledgling writer, whom he barely knew, under his wing. He became my mentor, advisor, and encourager. I thank you, Michael, from the bottom of my Southern heart.

Second is Gloria Pipkin, who is a local hero, for her untiring efforts against book censorship in our public schools over the past twenty-two years. Gloria was one of my first readers and she actually liked my book! Every time I wanted to give up, Gloria's words of encouragement kept me going.

I would also like to thank David Hancock, founder of Morgan James Publishing, Jim Howard, Ben Hancock and the entire Morgan James Publishing team for all their efforts in getting this book into print. Because of David's vision, many new writers are getting the opportunity to see their books published. No one could have been more encouraging or wonderful to work with than Jim and Ben is one of those delightful Southern gentlemen that every author should have the good fortune to cross paths. Last, but not least, many thanks to my ARM, Lyza Poulin, who gracefully kept everything and everyone on schedule.

For your enthusiasm, hard work, and belief in me, I give many thanks to my Panama City crew, Kathie, Kendall, Ruth, Elise, Bettina, and Linda.

Linda Moore a.k.a. Isabella is my muse. As a reader said, "Isabella lights up the pages" and Linda most definitely lights up my life. I could never ask for a better friend.

I am so grateful to have my Kappa Delta White Rose sisters in my life. Lois, Susan, Elizabeth, Tina, Kathy, Lynda, Ellen, and always, Barbara—you all know how crazy you are and you know how much I love you.

I am indebted to the many family and friends, past and present, who have waltzed through my life and make being a Southern so amusing. Most especially, I cherish the friendships I had with Pat and Kendall, whose love and spirit are with me every day.

Last, but certainly not least, I thank my husband Tommy, who truly is the funniest man I have ever met. During this entire process, he never once told me I was crazy and encouraged me every step of the way. To my son, Tommy Jr., who is my soul, I thank you for being the perfect son for me and giving me so much good material. And to my daughter, Elizabeth, who is my heart, my first reader, editor, and biggest cheerleader, you truly are the perfect daughter. I love you each.

Contents

Miss Hildreth Wore Brown

After many years away, one of my best friends recently moved back home to her small Southern town. One of her first duties was to accompany her mother to a funeral. Now funerals in the South are a serious business. They entail prodigious amounts of food, flowers, and family. My friend's mother is one of the greatest Southern ladies I have ever encountered. To be around her is to be in a perpetual state of amusement. One of her best friends and bridge partners, Miss Hildreth, had died. In the South, another important part of the funeral process is the viewing. You visit the funeral home, where there is an open casket, to pay your respects. Personally, I think the viewing ritual is unfair to the dead. Think about it. No matter what people say about you, you can't defend yourself. As my friend and her mother approached the casket, her mother looked down, threw her hands to her face, and exclaimed, "Oh dear Lawd! They put Miss Hildreth in brown. Brown is not her color. What were they thinking? Oh, Lawd!"

As my friend tells it, "It's so good to be back home. Is there any place like the South?"

Sassin'

I got exactly two spankings growing up. That's one more than my daughter got and 3,254 less than my son. I was reading an article in *Ladies Home Journal* that suggested you ask your children how you disciplined them. When I asked my daughter, she replied, "We sat down and talked about what I had done wrong, the consequences, and what a fair punishment would be." Well, I will have to admit, at this point, I was patting myself on the back thinking mother-of-the-year award. My son sauntered in and I asked him. He shrugged and answered, "You beat the crap out of me." So maybe not mother-of-the-year award. Before anyone calls the Department of Family Services and the child abuse investigators, my son does exaggerate—mightily. In fact, he is the king of hyperbole. I'm not here to argue the pros and cons of spanking, but when I grew up in the Old South the absolute cardinal sin was "sassin'"—the accounting of my two punishments. You did not under any circumstances talk back to your elders. Insolence in any form or fashion was not to be tolerated. It guaranteed a swift retribution normally in the form of a spanking.

I was in the grocery store the other day and a child of about three was begging his mother for a candy bar. Now I realize the candy aisle is a great temptation for a three-year-old but, in my way of thinking, you can't rid the world of all temptation so you may as well deal with it. For the umpteenth time, this young mother had very patiently—as the new generation of mothers is wont to do—told this little fellow he could not have the candy bar. She even tried to tell him why, using all the new techniques of child discipline floating around out there. Finally, he stomped his little foot and screamed, "No, I'm not listening to you!" and grabbed the candy bar. I thought, "O dear gussy, the wrath of God is about to descend on this little tot." I'm thinking murder on Aisle 10 of the Winn Dixie. Right? Wrong! In an exasperated voice the mother said, "Oh, all right, you can have it." I'm not lying. She actually said those words. The holy terror stuffed the candy in his mouth and three minutes later was begging for something else. I mean, why not? It worked so well the first time, he may as well go for the whole store.

Now I am certainly no authority on child discipline. My children erred in many and sundry ways and I often let them get away with things, but sassin' was not one of them. My generation learned early and thoroughly the no sassin' rule, and we felt it our birthright to pass it on to future generations. So, may I make a suggestion to all you young mothers out there since I expect you pretty much stick to the Ten Commandments, this being the Bible Belt and all. I exhort you to add "Thou Shalt Not Sass" to the list. It will save you heartbreak in the future and add years to your life.

Speaking of discipline, my favorite story comes from a friend who went temporarily insane and bore three children in four years. They were on a trip and it had been an especially trying twenty-four hours. The three cherubs were seated in the back of the car furiously trading insults when my friend finally snapped. She whipped around and pointing at each of them in turn said emphatically, "I hate you! I hate you! and I hate you!" Granted, this may not be the most positive form of discipline, but it worked. They are now three delightful adults with children of their own and they still talk about that momentous moment.

Another incident along these lines occurred on a trip with our young son. While we were traveling in the car, his behavior was becoming less and less desirable. Finally my son's shenanigans had gotten on my husband's last nerve, so he pulled the car onto the shoulder of the highway. As we had been on the road for some time, my husband had unbuckled his slacks to be more comfortable. He jumped out of the car—I assume to do combat with our son—and his pants fell down! I'm here to tell you, your sense of authority is greatly compromised when you are standing on the side of the road with your pants in a pile around your ankles.

While I am dishing out advice here, I want to throw in some about gratitude. When my son was ten, I accompanied him to a birthday party for one of his classmates. The birthday boy got a trillion dollar watch from his parents and immediately began whining because it lacked some particular feature. His mother clucked over him saying, "It's okay. We'll return this one and get you the watch you want." When we got in the car, I told my son if he ever acted that way I would take back every birthday gift he ever got and every one he was ever going to get. I mean even if you don't like a gift, you can show gratitude for the effort. In the South, in my day, gratitude was beaten into you. Nothing wrong with that I say!

Thank You Notes

I'll admit it. I have an obsession about writing thank you notes. I assume it's a Southern thing. My children swear I made them write a thank you note to our obstetrician for delivering them, all within twenty-four hours. Such hyperbole! I gave them a week. My all-time favorite thank you note came from a young bride whom we had given a fondue pot. She wrote, "Thank you for the nice gift. We have always wanted a pot of our own." In her defense, at least she wrote a thank-you note. Some of the ones I receive these days are scary. I expect to get one written on toilet paper any day now. When it comes to wedding gifts, I say if you're too busy to write thank you notes, you're too busy to get married.

I, for one, think the younger generation depends on computers entirely too much for this sort of thing. The other day my son actually wrote me a handwritten thank you note for a favor I had done for him. I'll admit I was mightily impressed. But he misspelled a word, and being a mother and a teacher, I felt it my obligation to point it out. To which he replied, "Funny, I wonder why spell check didn't catch that?"

Speaking of spell check, I really am totally dysfunctional when it comes to technology. The first time I tried to type a manuscript on the computer my son walked in while I was measuring the screen with a ruler. He totally fell out. Between gales of laughter he howled, "Why didn't Microsoft think of that? They could have included a ruler in every software package." Seems I was trying to center the title and all you had to do was click one little icon. Who knows these things anyway?

To illustrate how much stock I put in appropriate correspondence, one of my greatest compliments occurred when a good friend of my parents died. She came from a long line of grande dames. I was out of town and upon my return wrote the family a note of condolence. Her sister personally phoned me to express her thanks for the correspondence and to tell me how "beautifully executed" it was. I have to admit, happenstances like that just make me love the South!

I am obsessive about cards too. My husband wishes he had bought stock in Hallmark years ago. He says we could have retired by now.

After my daughter had been home visiting one weekend, the phone rang late Sunday night and she said, "Mom, I just walked into my apartment and was going through my mail. I left you approximately seven hours ago and my apartment is 1000 miles away. I just opened a card from you telling me how good I looked and how much fun we had this past weekend. Mom, when exactly did you mail this card?"

"Okay, okay, so maybe I did mail it before you ever got here. But I knew you would look good because you always do. And I knew we would have fun because we always have fun."

"Mom, I am not planning a wedding for the simple fact that I don't have a boyfriend. And because I'm not planning a wedding, I haven't picked out my china, silver, or crystal. But would it make you happy if I went ahead and wrote thank you notes for the wedding gifts I am going to receive?"

Oh the euphoria! She is my daughter after all.

Now my daughter does have a boyfriend and he was up for partner in his law firm. I had asked her to send me his mailing address. Knowing my penchant for cards and promptness, she sent me his address and added, in I thought a rather sarcastic tone, "Please wait until he actually makes partner before you send him a congratulations card." Not to be outdone, I wrote back, "Too late . . . congrats note already on its way . . . if he doesn't make partner just tell him to send it back . . . . Love, Mom."

Coffees And Coffee

I'm not positive about this (not having done the research) but I believe the morning social we call a coffee is a unique tradition of the South. A coffee is when a group of women get together to meet and greet a new bride, a pregnant bride (or these days maybe not yet a bride), a newcomer to town, a celebrity (which in our city would be the mayor's third cousin far removed), or the perpetual fundraiser. One coffee they cut a little close. The honoree went into labor and had to leave to deliver the little cherub. But she came right back to open all those gifts. She wasn't about to let a little thing like labor deter her from that stash of goodies.

You won't believe what happened the other day and this being the South it is most astonishing. My friend went to a coffee and there was no coffee. The hostess told her it was too hot. Well, the only thing that will keep my friend from killing someone when she hasn't had her coffee is chocolate, which she immediately went in search of only to be told by the same hostess it was too early for chocolate. My friend was speechless (as well as murderous) because she and I are in complete agreement on this. It is never too hot for coffee and never too early for chocolate. As she relayed to me, "I'll tell you one thing. Next coffee invitation I get, I'm calling to see if they're actually serving the stuff."

Speaking of coffee, my favorite thing in the world is to go to a little café, order doughnuts and coffee, read the paper and work the crossword puzzle. There is no television or telephone, but just peace and quiet. As all Americans can attest, there is now a Starbucks on every corner. I have never seen anything like it. But I personally don't want coffee that costs more than my children's first year college tuition. I don't want coffee that grows hair on your chest and under your armpits. Menopause does that. I also don't want hazelnut, vanilla, peppermint, or peach coffee. I just want a plain cup of coffee. Is that too much to ask? Apparently.

One of those fancy new coffee shops opened up, so I decided to give it a whirl. Of course, you have to wait in line forever while they ask if you want an espresso, mocha, cappuccino, latte, or low fat, nonfat, whole milk, or grande, short, tall. On my turn, I ordered coffee. The prepubescent girl behind the counter said, "Like, I don't think we have that."

"But this is a coffee shop," I practically screamed.

"Really," she said. "Who knew?"

So I ended up ordering a latte. Did you know a latte cost $3.95 and has 220 calories? (In the famous words of one prognosticator: No one will ever pay $3 for a cup of coffee. Tell Howard Schultz that!) A black cup of coffee, on the other hand, cost $1.10 and has zero calories. At this rate, this younger generation is going to be, like, fat and broke.

Who knew, indeed!

Chanel No. 5

My husband does not do malls. The last time he was in a mall my son was four-years-old and he took him Christmas shopping for my gifts. My son is about to draw Social Security, so you do the math. Okay, so I exaggerated a teeny bit, but you get the picture. Anyway, for some unknown reason, my husband decided to go for father-of-the-year award this particular year. With our four-year-old son in tow and my list, off they went.

After an hour or so, my son (who has been known to be a bit active) came bounding into the house shouting, "Mom, guess what we bought you."

"And spoil the surprise?" I asked.

Insisting he said, "Just guess one thing. It smells good."

"Perfume!" I ventured.

"Yes," he exclaimed. "It is Channel Number 5 (did I mention he watched the occasional TV) and, Mom, it cost $75.90 and Dad almost died!"

Well, I tell you, I had to laugh out loud. I knew my husband thought he was going in that store for a five dollar bottle of perfume. He had no clue women willingly took out loans for trifles such as fragrance. So here he is with his spirit-of-giving smile glued on, shelling out seventy-five big ones, all the while muttering under his breath about paying this much money for something that evaporates five minutes after you dab it on.

This became doubly humorous as the rest of the day was related to me. Our local Dairy Queen had been aggressively advertising their newest concoction named "The Blizzard," which our four-year-old had been begging to try. As the ad went, "The Blizzard" was made of ice cream so thick you could literally turn it upside down. So still working on the father-of-the-year award, my husband ended their little outing at the Dairy Queen. Much to my spouse's dismay, he soon discovered "The Blizzard" cost $2.95. For the second time that day he died, as he was still under the illusion a scoop of ice cream cost twenty-five cents. Exiting and grumbling mightily about the cost of paying almost three dollars for ice cream, our darling son spoke up, "But, Dad, the reason it cost so much is because it's so thick you can turn it upside down," and immediately preceded to demonstrate. Do the words "false advertising" ring a bell here? There is my husband, just having dished out $75 for perfume, looking at $3 worth of ice cream melting on the pavement at his feet.

I really got him good though. The day after Christmas, I faked spilling the entire bottle of Chanel No. 5. The man nearly had a coronary. I think he called the fire department. I couldn't help it. The devil made me do it. And him trying so hard to win father-of-the-year award!

Since my husband doesn't do malls, he doesn't do card shops either. Rather he fancies himself a Hallmark card writer. Either that or he hates paying $3.95 for a piece of paper you discard the next day. Regardless, every occasion I receive a homemade card from my husband. It has become his trademark. My all time favorite is the Valentine I opened a few years back. It had a stick figure Cupid running across the page. Written in red block letters inside a lopsided heart were the words, "I can think of 100 reasons why I love you." Upon opening the card, there lay a $100 bill with the message, "Don't you wish I could think of a million!"

Besides being a master of creating homemade cards, my husband also has a knack for turning a faux pas into a witticism. I suspect it comes from years of practice covering up his own personal gaffes.

We were at an exceptionally nice dinner party at the lovely home of friends. The wife had pulled out all the stops using her fine china and silver and crystal. It was a scrumptious gourmet meal. My husband is not known to be very discerning about food. In fact, he's so undiscerning he thinks I am a good cook, which works for me. I am certainly not a finicky eater but I do have my limits. I prefer to at least have a name for what I am putting in my mouth. Anyway, the salad course came and there was a strange-looking, I assumed vegetable, on my plate. Knowing my husband's penchant for eating anything, I asked him to sample this unknown food and tell me what it was. He gnawed for a few minutes then whispered, "Paper towel . . . Bounty."

I couldn't wait to get the hostess in the kitchen. We are very good friends and she is great fun. When I related this little tale, she howled, "I had a paper towel at the bottom of the greens and forgot about it. By the time I started to toss, it was too late. I just hoped no one would notice!" She was a great sport about the entire thing. I was preparing a Caesar salad the other night for dinner. I called to my husband, "Which do you want with your salad? Brawny or Bounty?"

"Surprise me," he said.

Directionally Challenged

E ven though we have lived in the South our whole lives, my entire family cannot tell north from south. To say we are directionally challenged, in today's lingo, is an understatement. When my son was about ten, I was taking him to play in a soccer match in Niceville, Florida. For the record, Florida is the state we reside in. My husband was staying home with our daughter and to my credit, as I was driving off just to be certain, I asked him if I took State Road 79. Being the detailed-oriented male he is, he replied, "Yes." (See Chapter on Details.) About an hour later my son and I see the state sign for Alabama! I knew immediately this was not good. My son thought it was the neatest thing since they invented white bread. I stopped at the first country store I came to which was an exact scene from *My Cousin Vinny*, with three very elderly gentlemen rocking on the front porch. When I explained my predicament, the first gentleman said wryly, "You're trying to get to Florida and you're headed toward Alabama. I'd say you're lost little lady." I wanted to snap back, "Really old codger, what gives you that idea!" Being the polite Southern girl my parents raised, I just replied, "If you could point me in the right direction, I'd sure appreciate it." At that point, a lengthy discussion ensued, as all three old gentlemen had the best route on how to return me to the Sunshine State.

All I know, I eventually got my son to his soccer game at half time. As things go, the opposing team was beating the tar out of us so it wouldn't have mattered whether he showed up or not. My son was so amused by the little fact we went to Alabama instead of Florida, he ran shouting from the car to anyone who would listen, "My mom drove us to Alabama!" I'm so proud he shared that little bit of information for the world to know.

It's always nice for as many people as possible to know how dumb you are. Quite frankly, I had planned on keeping it a secret. When we got home, I inquired of my husband why he didn't deem it important to tell me to turn west onto Highway 20 from State Road 79. "Didn't think you'd know which direction west was," is all he said. That's the last time I'll use him for a map.

I remember the day I realized this direction deficiency was genetic. It was the day that I picked my ten-year-old nephew up from school. One of my nephew's passions is fishing and he couldn't wait to go fishing in the bayou behind our house. My sister had asked me to take him to the Bee Line convenience store to get bait or lures or whatever fishermen need. I told my nephew he was going to have to give me directions to the Bee Line as I'd never been there. Being a man of few words, he confidently replied, "Sure." My nephew, being an exceptionally polite, patient young man, began giving me very methodical directions. I did notice we were going back toward his house, thinking maybe he had forgotten something. But, no, from his house he continued with directions until we arrived at the Bee Line, which happened to be right next door to his school! When I mentioned this fact, he replied, "I only know the directions from my house."

All I can say is what can you do with errant DNA? Honestly, if I were a gene, I would be the directionally challenged one just for the pure amusement.

My daughter and I have traveled quite a lot together and she always says, "If you don't get lost on a trip, you're not traveling with Mom." On one occasion, we were driving from Williamsburg, Virginia, into Washington, D.C. I was so proud of myself. I had purchased a Washington, D.C. map before we left home and perfectly mapped out the route to the rental car return. I'd even planned it for a Sunday to avoid downtown D.C. traffic. I soon discovered one small problem. I had used the subway lines on the map instead of the streets. Did you know the subway in Washington, D.C., does not end at Avis Rental Car? Well, you know it now. My eight-year-old learned a few new words that momentous day. Words that most likely won't be on the SAT. But, honestly, do you blame me? I mean I had actually tried to find my way.

My husband can't say a word. He is every bit as bad as I am when it comes to directions. We had the same babysitter for six years and every time—and I do mean every time—we took our son to her house he drove right past it. He'd mumble something about she moved her mailbox again. Now I ask you, how many times do people actually move their mailbox?

One time I was driving us to our favorite oyster bar. Note the operative word here "favorite," which correctly implies we had frequented it many times before. My husband insisted, and I mean adamantly insisted, I had passed it. I made him bet me one hundred dollars. I never had so much fun spending a hundred dollars in my life. If you know for a fact you can't tell north from south, why on earth would you bet money on it? He deserved to lose is all I can say.

Southern Grandmothers

I had two wonderful Southern grandmothers. My maternal grandmother, Mama Ruby, lived in Gainesville, Georgia, in a little white wooden house with green shutters on Chandler Street. As a young child, I would spend two weeks every summer with her. My mind can still walk through that house on Chandler Street like it was yesterday. It was the kind of neighborhood where you roamed free looking for four-leaf clovers in the daytime and catching fireflies in jars with hole-punched lids at night. Mama Ruby was a large, cushioned woman who loved to swoop down and wrap you against her breasts in her warm arms. She was a gregarious, loving lady with a ready laugh, who had borne nine children. Granddaddy, on the other hand, was a wiry, taciturn sort. My main recollection of him is at breakfast time. Every single morning, Mama Ruby would line four fruit glasses in front of his place. They were those old-fashioned glasses with pictures of sundry fruit decoupages on the front. He would drink orange juice, grapefruit juice, prune juice, and buttermilk, in that order. I was both fascinated and thankful I didn't have to partake in this ritual, especially drinking the disgusting prune juice not to mention the odorous buttermilk.

Mama Ruby's favorite friend in the whole world was Mrs. McClure. She and Mr. McClure lived across Chandler Street in a house with an awning that had an "M" embellished on it. I found that awning rather quaint. Mr. and Mrs. McClure loved my younger sister and me almost as much as my grandparents loved us. They had, what was to my young eyes, a humongous screened-in back porch bordered by woods. Mr. McClure would set up the porch like a campsite and my sister and I would rough it for the night which usually entailed eating peanut butter and jelly sandwiches and playing cards with Mr. McClure until we dozed off. Mr. McClure taught me these really neat card tricks and to this day he is a magician in my eyes.

Mama Ruby was of the generation that spent a great deal of their day in the kitchen. In my mind, my grandmother will always be wearing an apron with a dish towel permanently attached to her right hand. The absolute highlight of Mama Ruby and Mrs. McClure's day came at one thirty in the afternoon with their favorite soap opera "As the World Turns." That globe would appear on the screen and they dropped everything and came running. They lived vicariously through Claire and James and all the other characters that paraded across the black and white television set. If you think they sat demurely and took it all in, you would be wrong. They'd jump up and shout, "You brazen hussy, what are you doing stealing her husband," or "Harlot, get away from that man. He's already taken." Then Mama Ruby would use that permanently attached dish towel like Zorro and start swishing it at the TV. Every time a character misbehaved, she'd swat harder. I thought it the greatest fun in the world and my vocabulary was immensely enriched.

One summer a youngish divorcee rented the house next door to Mama Ruby. The first day she pranced out wearing skin tight short shorts—Daisy Dukes as they are known today—and from that day on she was the strumpet next door. Like I said, my vocabulary was greatly enhanced those summers. I could have told that poor woman the minute she walked out in those Daisy Dukes she never stood a chance in that neighborhood. My preacher uncle, wife, and children were visiting that particular summer. One day the divorcee came over, quite upset because her children's cat had gotten on the roof. She pleaded with my uncle to climb up a ladder and rescue their cat. Mama Ruby had one hissy fit. She exhorted my uncle not to get up on that ladder and break his neck for that "lady of the night, that concubine who lived in a den of iniquity." Not surprisingly, Mama Ruby was always drawn to the soap opera parts of the Bible. My uncle was the tenderest of men and a preacher to boot, so of course, he got the cat down. I can still see Mama Ruby slamming the screen door, stomping in the house, grumbling all the while, and swishing that dish towel to beat the band. We all got out of her path that day in case she missed and then you'd sho' 'nuff be slapped up side the head!

During some of my most formative years, I was raised by my paternal grandmother, Mama Byrd. I am named after her, and of all the things I was endowed without choice, my name is my most special gift. It darn sure beats my nose! I have always loved my name and I know it is directly related to my adoration for my grandmother. She was the greatest of Southern ladies, a study in dichotomies. She was resilient but flexible; tough yet kind; self-assured while unselfish; religious and spiritual. I am what I am today largely because of Mama Byrd, and not so much because of what she said but more the life she lived. She was witty, intelligent, and a lifelong teacher.

Some of my favorite childhood memories are playing cards, board games, and "quizzes" with Mama Byrd. There is one small problem in this respect. I absolutely hate to lose. My children are quite competitive and they unequivocally blame me. It seems I never "let" them win at Candy Land. I say you win fair and square or you don't win, even if you are six months old. The first time they both beat me at Scrabble, in the same game I might add, they pulled out the champagne and celebrated for a week. This brings me to the point my children were of drinking age before they managed to beat me at Scrabble. Nevertheless, I was none too happy, I'll tell you. My son won with the word "erg." For the next year, I received clever little emails like "ergs" to you, blah, blah, ad nauseum. You get the picture. To really rub it in, the children gave me a Scrabble calendar for Christmas, so I could "practice for our next game" as the card so candidly put it. Such clever children I have raised.

One of Mama Byrd's dearest friends from her younger days was a lady we called Aunt Jolly. In the South, it seems sooner or later everyone becomes your aunt. Mama Byrd and Jolly were young school teachers together in Enterprise, Alabama. Aunt Jolly married and had a baby ten months later. Tragically, her husband was killed in a train accident when her baby daughter was only a month old. Mama Byrd always woefully commented Aunt Jolly was a bride, a mother, and a widow all in less than a year. Aunt Jolly confided to my grandmother that she was never marrying again. She had her daughter and she had no intention of breeding children the rest of her life. She was true to her word and dedicated her life to the classroom students who passed her way. Her daughter, Claire, became one of my surrogate mothers.

Part of our family lore is the day my father took my grandmother to renew her driver's license. She was eighty-nine years old and everybody except Mama Byrd knew she didn't need to be on the road behind the wheel of a car. She wasn't about to relinquish that driver's license voluntarily, I can tell you that. She was most nervous about the eye exam. The instructor asked my grandmother to read the eye chart and she passed with flying colors so she was feeling somewhat better about the whole process. Then he asked her to cover her right eye with her hand. "Can you read the chart now?" he asked.

"No," she replied rather peevishly, "and I don't drive this way either!"

With that, I think the instructor just renewed her license anyway. Mama Byrd continued to drive until the automatic bar at the drawbridge crashed into her windshield. She never heard the rather loud bells or saw the bar coming! With that, even my indomitable grandmother realized it was time to quit the highways.

So here's my advice to all you young women out there. Find yourself a true Southern woman to emulate. Let her become your mentor. Your life will be hugely enriched and you will always be amused. So I say "ergs" to you Mama Byrd and Mama Ruby. I was one lucky Southern woman.

Great-Aunt Lottie Mae

Other regions have their interesting people, but the South has its characters. My Great-Aunt Lottie Mae was one such character. According to the town grapevine, she adored her husband, who was mayor of our fair city. They lived in an elegant antebellum home surrounded by graceful Southern oaks and magnolias. They had no children, so Aunt Lottie's house, as well as her nieces and nephews, became her pride and joy. She traveled the world and filled her home with antiques and oriental rugs and silver and crystal. I spent quite a bit of time in that house as a child. Unfortunately, her husband died of a sudden heart attack at an early age, as the town gossips declared he was the one person who could keep Lottie Mae "in line."

Aunt Lottie was as old-fashioned and opinionated as the day is long. She believed women should never, absolutely never, wear pants. And from as early an age as I can remember she was always saying, "You have to be careful of men. They only want one thing." I heard that constantly from childhood on and had no clue what Aunt Lottie was talking about. But I'm here to tell you, it was a red letter day when I discovered what that "one thing" was! Her other favorite mantra was, "You can love someone rich as easy as you can love someone poor." As a young teenager, I would roll my eyes at the unfairness of that statement. Now I tell my daughter, "You can love someone rich as easy as you can love someone poor!"

When my stepmother came into our lives, I could have told her she never had a chance with Aunt Lottie, but I figured she'd find out soon enough. Sure enough, my stepmother stripped a piece of mahogany furniture Aunt Lottie had given us years ago and stained it white. Aunt Lottie vowed to never set foot in our house again. Secretly, I think my stepmother did it on purpose to take care of Aunt Lottie once and for all.

Aunt Lottie was the only Southern woman I know who could get away with calling people a jackass, and she did so liberally. My mother certainly taught us it was unladylike and improper. But since in those days I never heard women swear, I thought it hilarious. At one time or another, everybody was a jackass to Aunt Lottie. I can imagine the lawyer's face when she flew into his office to strike yet another jackass off her will.

I personally never knew Aunt Lottie to enter the inside of a church though I guess she did get married in one. She started threatening to leave her house to the church. The whole town thought she was bluffing as religious matters had never seemed that important to her. Well, Aunt Lottie Mae showed us all. Unfortunately, around seventy-five years of age she "lost her marbles," as we so picturesquely say in the South. It is called Alzheimer's today. Aunt Lottie lived about fifteen more years. There were three heirs left in her will that somehow had escaped jackass classification. She did indeed leave her antebellum house to the church. I don't know who was laughing harder, God or Aunt Lottie.

I would be remiss if I did not pay homage to several other characters of our quaint town. One woman is not old enough to yet be considered a character, but when she reaches the appropriate age I am quite sure she will be dubbed such. Sister was born and bred in Eufaula, Alabama, so she is steeped in the traditions and lore of the Old South. She is called Sister because she is an only girl with four brothers. We take our names literally in the South! Sister is an ardent horsewoman and she and her husband reside in an elegant English house surrounded by acres of property. She has parlayed this passion for horses into creating one of the premier horse shows of our region.

We were at her home for our town's annual library fundraiser. I was gaily chatting with one of the authors when, lo and behold, Sister rides into the living room on a horse! Now let me assure you this was not a pony. This was a full grown horse. As you might imagine, this happening was the topic of conversation for the remainder of the evening. As I was standing near the bar, I heard the bartender quip to a gentleman, "I had to cut the last fellow off. He swore he saw a horse in the house!"

One character who would be offended if she were not mentioned is Mrs. Brewton, a quintessential Southern dame who sat on the front row of the local church. Mrs. Brewton's trademarks were her turbans and dark sunglasses. From childhood into adulthood, I was eternally fascinated by her turbans. You never saw Mrs. Brewton without these head coverings and they always matched her attire perfectly down to the identical fabric. It was a mystery to everyone how she pulled that off. Add to that Marlene Dietrich sunglasses and you had quite a picture. I realize Marlene Dietrich eyewear is back in vogue but Mrs. Brewton wore those sunglasses rain, sun, snow, sleet, inside, outside, regardless of vogue. She also called everyone "dahling" whether they were darling or not.

Mr. and Mrs. Brewton were no longer able to take care of their antebellum home, so they moved to a fifth floor condominium. As folk lore goes, Mr. Brewton died and when the funeral director came he realized the gurney was too long to put in the elevator. So he strapped Mr. Brewton on that gurney and stood it up for the ride down. As the elevator doors opened, a neighbor spied the Brewtons and greeted them, to which Mrs. Brewton famously replied, "Oh, no, dahling! He's dead!"

Last, but certainly not least of these great Southern characters, is my neighbor who is the grandest of Southern ladies. Besides looking like she stepped out of *Vogue* magazine, she is a Bible whiz with a marvelous sense of humor who is the first to laugh at herself. She is barely

five feet in stature and at ninety-four years of age still
wears four inch stiletto heels, as she swears it is the only
way she can walk. There is a new race in Europe called
"Stiletto Run," in which women run a race in three and
one-half inch heels to win a $15,000 shopping spree. I
guarantee my neighbor would leave those young gals in
a trail of dust.

My neighbor also sits on the front row of our local
church. Each Fourth of July, the church pays tribute
to our armed forces by singing the song of each service
branch, at which time those who have served in that
particular branch stand. It really is quite moving. My
neighbor happened to doze off this particular July Fourth
and suddenly awoke to the singing of "From the Halls of
Montezuma." Hearing music, she immediately popped
up on her feet. Her friend whispered incredulously, "I
didn't know Vivian was in the Marines!"

I can only assume that in other parts of the country
people do not ride a full grown horse through the living
room at their little soirees, converse with the dead on
elevators, or have nonagenarians serving in the Marines.
I have to believe it is the kind of occurrences that only
happen in the South. But, honestly, I ponder these things.
I surely do.

Mrs. Bell

There is no shortage of surrogate mothers in the South. You may not have a mother, but you are never motherless. Mrs. Bell was one of those surrogate mothers for me. She was my grandmother's best friend, and I loved her. She was a very tall, large-boned woman (that is not a euphemism for fat). Like many Southern women she was known to be quite tenacious (that is a euphemism for just plain stubborn). One of Mrs. Bell's greatest joys in life was singing in the church choir and, with her size, she had a pair of lungs to prove it.

On this particular Sunday, we were having the worship service in the close quarters of the Fellowship Hall since the church was in the progress of building a new sanctuary. Normally we always stand when we sing hymns, but the Minister of Music had decided to sit this one out. As we began the hymn, Mrs. Bell popped up out of the choir, the only human standing in the entire choir and congregation. Now most people at this juncture would show embarrassment, hastily retreat, sit down, and hope only a few people noticed. Not Mrs. Bell. She pulled herself to her full height, impressive as it was, belted out that hymn with those powerful lungs, all the while glowering at the hapless Minister of Music. Our Minister of Music was a short, slight man, and I think he must have known what was coming because as soon as the service was over he made a beeline for the nearest exit. To this day, I have a visual image of Mrs. Bell hightailing it after him, choir robe flowing and finger wagging, telling him she was positive he told us to stand for that hymn. Never mind five hundred church members and fifty choir members remained seated.

One of the first things you learn in the South is that it's fruitless to argue with a Southern woman like Mrs. Bell. Love her as we did, quite simply, she was always right and never wrong.

Success

I had an experience in my childhood that left a vivid impression on me all these many years. We all know in this generation there has been a plethora of advice on raising children and the importance of self-esteem. A virtual smorgasbord of ideas has been thrown out on the best way to instill self-esteem in children.

I had an aunt who lived in Jefferson City, Missouri, who had six boys and one girl, and every summer they came to spend two weeks with Aunt Lottie Mae. This family will always be special to me. The first Christmas after my mother died Aunt Lottie took me and my younger sister on the overnight train to Missouri to spend the holidays with them. That alone was a thrill for a five and ten-year-old. St. Louis was tinseled like a Winter Wonderland and all the store windows animated with Mr. and Mrs. Clauses, dancing elves, and flying reindeer. It snowed one day and we rode sleds, which was quite a treat for children from the Sunshine State.

Spending Christmas with a brood of seven was grand fun. David was the cousin my age, and I was in my basketball phase, so of course, that delighted him.

We thoroughly enjoyed each other's young company. My aunt, uncle, and cousins turned what could have been a dismal Christmas into a magical one.

The next summer when these cousins came to visit Aunt Lottie, I was in my miniature golf phase. In Florida, we called it putt-putt golf. I believe I have alluded to my competitive nature, so I tackled putt-putt golf like Arnold Palmer. I was in a perpetual contest to beat my own score as well as everyone else's. When David came that summer, I got a brainstorm to build a miniature golf course in our back yard. I always was one for grandiose ideas! David and I developed a blueprint and calculated we had room for four golf holes. There was a section of our yard shaded by huge oak trees, thus no grass grew, so we were given permission to dig away. We purloined old bricks piled by the side of the house for the borders. We even angled some to give it creativity. We used Maxwell House coffee cans dug into the ground for the holes and got rather fanciful with "sand traps" and "bunkers." We talked my grandmother out of a tin wash tub and finagled a water hazard.

It took David and me a good part of a week to construct our putt-putt course and, if I do say so myself, it was quite a feat for two ten-year-olds. I can vividly recall to this day the immense pride I had in that accomplishment. I felt we had achieved the neatest thing in the world. And the best part, other than begging a washtub, we did the entire project without any adult interference. We confiscated some putters and golf balls, and David and I spent the next week delightedly playing putt-putt golf on our homemade course. I even let him beat me a few times! David had to return home to Jefferson City, and the rains eventually came and washed our course away. But it didn't matter. The sense of pride was a part of me forever. There wasn't a rain hard enough to wash that away.

This is my way of thinking about that experience after all this time. You can tell children they are intelligent or beautiful or talented all you want, but that doesn't give them self-esteem. Self-esteem comes from trying and failing and finally succeeding. It comes from your own efforts and not those of your parents. That's just how I see it these many years later.

Victoria's Secret

I walked into a Victoria's Secret with my daughter the other day. Now I know I am no spring chicken here, and I'm not about to publish my age for all the world to see, but I don't have a foot in the grave yet either. After five minutes in Victoria's Secret, I felt like I had been living in a cocoon.

Did you realize fishnet hose have gone mainstream? When my daughter asked what exactly I meant, I said, "It means not just strippers wear them." Can you Southern women out there imagine such! My Great-Aunt Lottie Mae is not only turning over in her grave, but so is my whole line of Southern ancestors. And, another thing, everywhere I looked there were thongs. I can tell you right here and now, if you ever catch me in a pair of thongs, you will know I am in the last stages of Alzheimer's.

Immediately upon entering the store, you are greeted with a video on one wall. I don't mean a nice little twenty-six inch television screen, but an entire wall. Now I am not making this up. I don't have near enough imagination to make this one up. One of the models was at least seven foot two inches tall with seven feet of legs. Have you ever

41

seen a five foot two inch model? I didn't think so. She had more hair than Rapunzel. Her attire, if that is what you could call it, was a leopard skin bra (probably killed a whole leopard for two inches of fabric) and underwear so brief Webster doesn't have a word for it yet. On one side, coming out of the bra was a gigantic ostrich feather held in place with a rhinestone pin. This model had on a leather belt with a large buckle. Now I ask you. This woman is practically nude. What exactly is that leather belt holding up?

This ensemble was finished off with my all-time favorite—a pair of neon pink and purple-striped leg warmers topped off with suede moccasin boots tied by straps up to the knees. I may not speak for all Southern men of my generation, but I do believe if my husband was presented with this apparition, he would duck into the nearest dressing room. Okay, the bra and pants I can see, but where was I when leg warmers became sexy? That settles it. I'm headed back to my cocoon where I sincerely pray my husband will join me.

Hair

I don't know what it is about Southern women and their hair, but we are neurotic. One hundred per cent humidity and hair is a very challenging combination. I was at a luncheon the other day, and every woman there had gorgeous hair. I wanted to snatch every one of them bald, and these are my friends. Just shows you what bad hair will do to you. There was Elizabeth, a beautiful ash blonde, who has never, and I mean never, had a bad hair day in her entire life. Across the table sat Martha with a head of shiny, bouncy hair. She is one of those disgusting women who could have done a Prell commercial. Next to me was Ellen with thick, wavy blonde hair, pure sickening.

Then there's me. There are only three words to describe my hair—fine, fine, and fine. I have a hate-hate relationship with my hair. The way I see it, I devote entirely too much time and money to these tresses for the return on my dollar. You women with thick, gorgeous hair can skip this chapter. But you soul sisters with fine hair can read on. I have tried every kind of shampoo known to woman. I've gelled, moussed, shellacked, and sprayed.

I've used blow dryers, curling irons, electric curlers with and without mist, straighteners, and foam rollers. In college, I even slept in wire and bristle curlers which, needless to say, was pure agony! Talk about desperate to get a husband.... Sometimes I think the only reason I got married was so I wouldn't have to torture myself in those wire curlers. I probably shouldn't share that little fact with my husband.

When I go to get my hair styled (my dear friend Kendall called it a hairdo instead of a hair style but then again she was raised in Moultrie, Georgia), I'm positive my stylist Joe is grimacing because he's thinking she's going to want me to do the opposite of what I did last time, which is the same as I did the time before and frankly, my dear, it isn't going to matter. But Joe just swirls me in that chair and says rather tongue-in-cheek, "Sure, honey, we'll try it. I'm positive you'll look just like Julia Roberts."

Someone had mentioned I looked like Sally Fields in those Boniva commercials she's been doing of late. Must be a rude awakening to go from the Academy Awards to hanging around orthopedic clinics, but then such is life even for the rich and famous. So I asked Joe if he thought I favored Sally Fields. Joe, who isn't known for his tactfulness, love him as we do, just said, "She's been pulled tighter." Translation: Sally Fields looks young; you on the other hand, look old. I guess it comes as no surprise the sign on Joe's mirror says "Sarcasm: Just One More Service We Offer Here."

One time, my daughter asked me if I liked using all that hair spray. With not a little bit of sarcasm, I replied, "Sure, I love cleaning three inches of goop off my bathroom counter everyday. And I love going around looking like Sally Fields in *Steel Magnolias* with a football helmet glued on my head." But what choice do I have? As I noted, one hundred per cent humidity and fine hair are a sure recipe for disaster.

I made a New Year's resolution this year to get over my hair. It is what it is. It ain't gonna change. I was in the grocery check-out line the other day perusing the headlines of major world events like "Brittany Spears Has Baby by Aliens" when I saw a model on a magazine cover with the cutest hair style. Before I knew it I'm thinking, maybe, just maybe this time. Let's face it. When it comes to Southern women and their hair, hope springs eternal! I'm pretty sure my demise will come from hair spray inhalation trying to look like Julia Roberts.

Weddings

I woke up the other morning, took one look in the mirror, and went and called my children. "You have to get married. My face is falling. People are going to think I'm the grandmother of the bride/groom instead of the mother, for Pete's sake! Do you really want me walking down the aisle on a walker with oxygen attached?" The last time my son had a girlfriend and met her mother, the first words out of my mouth were, "How old does she look?" Not, is she a nice person or even is she sane? The other day a friend asked me if my son was dating anyone special. "No, "I replied, "but I'm down to anyone who's not a hooker." One friend inquired about recovering hookers. I told her I'd have to get back to her on that one. But giving it some thought, people deserve a second chance, don't you think?

The other Sunday my son was in the church parking lot and an elderly couple rammed into the rear of his car. The gentleman was attempting to act like it wasn't his fault, but his wife wasn't about to let that happen. She was a regular magpie and got out of the car just a-fussing, "I told him he better look in his rear view mirror. I knew he wasn't paying attention." Then she got a glimpse of my son and stopped midsentence. "You're so cute!" she exclaimed.

"Thank you, ma'am," my son politely replied.

"Are you single?" she asked.

"Yes, ma'am."

"Are you gay?"

"No, ma'am."

"Well, I have just the girl for you. She is a waitress at our favorite restaurant. She has an adorable three-year-old child and she is just the cutest thing. You two would be perfect for each other."

I've been trying to find a wife for my son for thirty-one years. It took this lady thirty seconds. What do I know? I'm only the mother. If any of you northern boys are having trouble finding a wife, ya'll just move to the South. You can find them in the most unexpected places.

Has anyone else noticed how this new generation dates ten years before they get married? Often they cohabit five of those years. I heard about a couple who dated ten years, got married, and divorced six months later. Is there anyone out there who understands this? What exactly did they learn about each other in six months that they didn't figure out in ten years? I mean if you're an axe murderer how long can you disguise it? I say marry them before you find out about all those annoying and idiosyncratic habits that drive you slap-dab crazy. Preferably have children and seal the deal. I even go so far as to say if the

couple doesn't stay married at least a year, demand your
wedding gift back.

Okay, I admit my generation didn't have all the answers
and we might have been a bit hasty. Maybe I didn't learn
my husband's last name until we were applying for the
marriage license. Now I love my husband to pieces, but all
you women of my generation I ask you. If you knew what
you know now, would you be so quick to stand up in front
of God and three hundred witnesses (so you can't plead
ignorance) and promise to honor and obey (obey?—what
were we thinking), in sickness and in health, for richer
or for poorer (poorer?—really, what were we thinking),
until death do us part. And let's talk about this death part.
Every time I pick up the newspaper, they've added two
years to the life expectancy. I mean this death thing is
getting to be serious business. Think about it. Every time
you read the newspaper, you're married longer.

When this new generation finally does get married,
am I the only one out there who notices the bride and
groom never leave the reception anymore? In my day, we
poked cake in each other's mouth, ate a chicken wing,
drank a glass of champagne, and went off to do you
know what. Nowadays, I can't remember the last time I
outlasted the bride and groom.

One thing this generation does better at weddings
is those little bottles of bubbles. All that rice we threw,
probably the cause of global warming! The problem
is you aren't supposed to blow those bubbles until the

happy couple leaves, which as far as I can tell, they never do. Well, I love to blow those little bottles of bubbles. It's the highlight of the wedding to me. Am I the only who has gone up to the bridal couple and asked, "Don't you two want to have sex any time tonight?" I can only assume when you've been dating for ten years the luster of sex has kind of worn thin.

The only thing I have to say to my children is why are you waiting? He or she is not going to change. I even have evidence of this fact. In a Dear Abby letter I just read, a guest had been to a formal family wedding where the groom was so intoxicated the bride had to hold him up during the ceremony for him to repeat his vows. Here's the clincher. They had dated for ten years! If you don't think that's proof they're not going to change, then you're living under a rock. So, please, listen to voices of experience. At this rate, my face lift is going to cost more than your weddings.

Since my daughter now has a boyfriend, I thought it fair game to talk about weddings, at least in theory. I was mentioning some people we would invite and she said, "Mom, I don't know those people."

"And your point would be?"

She just stared at me.

"Whose wedding is this anyway?" I asked.

She just stared at me.

"Okay, you can pick out the colors for the bridesmaid dresses. Just make it pale aqua or mint green."

She just stared at me.

"Next thing I know you're going to want to pick out the groom."

She just stared at me.

"That was a joke. Where's your sense of humor? If you're going to plan a wedding, you have to have a sense of humor."

"We'll talk about this when you come to your senses," she said as she exited the room.

Little does my daughter know what little sense I ever did possess went with childbirth. So obviously we won't be having this conversation again. It's okay. I'll just plan her wedding and hope she shows up. But I'll tell you one thing—if she does show up, she's leaving that reception. If I have to pay for a wedding, I'm darn sure blowing those little bubbles.

Robert Redford

Southerners are supposed to do everything slowly. It's in our genes. I have a dry-witted friend from the North (another name for a smart aleck) who interrupts me while I'm talking and so cleverly says, "Now, how many syllables are in that word?" I want to respond, "Well at least you know it's a word. You, on the other hand, talk so fast it sounds like you're speaking a foreign language." Being the polite Southern lady I was raised to be, I restrain myself and just smile. But nothing in my upbringing keeps me from thinking it.

I read about an experiment that was done with theology students. They had just studied the parable of the Good Samaritan in the New Testament. These students were given a task to accomplish and given varying times to complete it. Then a homeless man was planted in their path. Personally, I call this entrapment. Anyway, the students who had the most time to complete the task by and large stopped to help the homeless man. Those in a hurry by and large did not.

No surprise here. When I have time, I'm the most gracious Southern thing you've ever met. Waiting in a line, I'll chat about the weather, your attire, or any other major world event that comes up. I can prattle inanely with the best of them. But if I'm running late, woe to the person who gets in my way.

This is never more evident than when I'm going to a movie. I am a movie aficionado (okay, an addict) and there is absolutely no way I'm going to miss the beginning of a movie. I've been known to run over little old ladies with oxygen tanks if they're blocking my way. And let's talk about the popcorn line. If someone's taking too long getting their money out or is ordering half the concession stand, I truly want to strangle them. "Sorry, Judge, but they took too long to pay for their popcorn. Surely you understand. The movie was starting."

Anyway, as I was saying, I'm a movie addict. And what's a movie without popcorn, even if I have to kill for it. Now don't start bellyaching about the cost of drinks and popcorn at a movie nowadays. If I have to ransom my first child to keep movie theaters in business, so be it. My friend Kendall called it a picture show, but I think I mentioned she was bred in Moultrie, Georgia.

To illustrate how crazed I am concerning movies, the other day two older women stopped me outside the movie theater to ask if I had seen any of the films now playing. They were debating between *The Other Boleyn Girl* and *Bank Job*. I immediately commented what a wonderful movie *The Other Boleyn Girl* was and then launched into a dissertation on Henry VIII and his six wives. I proceeded to inform them that, in my humble opinion, Anne Boleyn was one of the most underrated women in history. I mean after all, she was one of the main reasons England is a Protestant nation, not to mention the fact she gave birth to one of the most famous of all English monarchs, Queen Elizabeth I. At last as I took a breath, I noticed these two ladies eyes were glazed over and their mouths agape. Finally one of the women muttered, "Is it boring?"

"On second thought," I answered, "you might enjoy *Bank Job* more." In hindsight, I realize these nice ladies possibly just wanted a simple movie suggestion and not a thirty minute history lecture on the Tudors.

I remember vividly to this day the first movie I ever saw, *Song of the South*. I bawled my eyes out when they banished Uncle Remus. And what woman hasn't watched Mr. Darcy stride across the English countryside in *Pride and Prejudice* and thought, "I was definitely born in the wrong century." I settle down into the dark aura of a movie theater and I am transported to another time and place.

I am Meryl Streep in *Out of Africa* with Robert Redford. You know which scene—the one in the tent. Use your imagination here. I am Barbra Streisand in *The Way We Were* with Robert Redford. She finally hooks up with the college hunk. Okay, he was drunk and doesn't remember a thing, but let's not get picky. I am Katherine Ross in *Butch Cassidy and the Sundance Kid* with Robert

Redford. You know where he holds a gun on her in the bedroom scene, but he isn't really holding a gun on her. I guess that's cowboy foreplay. I am Jane Fonda in *Barefoot in the Park* with Robert Redford. In my opinion, the elevator send-off is one of the best scenes in filmdom. Honestly, I have always wanted to do that and I don't even care with whom. I am Kristin Scott Thomas in the *Horse Whisperer* with Robert Redford dancing on the ranch. Who needs sex when you can dance like that? I am Demi Moore in *Indecent Proposal* with Robert Redford and we all know where that goes.

Okay, so you've noticed a small pattern here. It's true. I have this "thing" for Robert Redford. I know the exact moment it transpired. It was in the dark ambience of the Martin Theatre. I was sixteen-years-old watching *This Property Is Condemned* starring Natalie Wood and Robert Redford. I've never gotten over it. Now I know what you're thinking, but my husband (who we've already ascertained I love to pieces) knows all about Robert Redford and he is perfectly fine with it. A little make-believe never hurt anybody he says.

You won't believe this, but I almost met Robert Redford. Notice I said almost. If my daddy hadn't raised such a polite Southern girl, I would have. I was visiting my daughter in Washington, D.C., and had gone to pick her up from work. I was waiting in a small reception area reading the paper when out walked my daughter's boss with Robert Redford. I had met her boss only briefly a few months prior, so of course he didn't recognize me. I had my moment to get up and reintroduce myself, but my Southern demureness kicked in, and I saw my golden moment fleeting before my eyes. At that minute, I could have kicked my daddy for making sure I never interrupted adults. You'd think by middle age I would have gotten over that, but apparently some lessons stick for life. Anyway, they talked about five minutes and I want you to know I was practically in cardiac arrest, but being the Southern woman I am, I stayed as cool as a cucumber and never even broke a sweat. They headed toward the door and this is the gospel truth. Robert Redford turned, looked straight at me, said hello, and smiled! Since the boss was out the door and we can be absolutely positive Robert Redford has no recollection of the moment, God is my witness that's exactly how it happened.

When my daughter's boss came back into the reception area, then of course, I introduced myself to which he replied, "I'm sorry I didn't recognize you. I could have introduced you to Robert Redford." I wanted to fall in a puddle and wail but, of course, being the Southern lady I am, I just smiled like it was perfectly fine. When he got back to his office, he told my daughter, "I think I just make a big mistake. I didn't recognize your mother so I didn't introduce her to Robert Redford."

"That's okay," my daughter quipped, "I'm pretty sure you'll get credit for a sighting!"

Just for the record, I'm not awed by just any ole movie star. I have my standards. Robert Redford has my admiration because he has spent a large portion of his life as an advocate for the environment and independent film makers. So you see I'm not shallow. There is depth to my lust.

The Devil Is In The Details

Southern women talk slow and in detail. Men, on the other hand, no matter where they're from, tell you exactly nothing. I would ask my daughter about her school day and she'd tell me how many times her teacher went to the bathroom. I'd ask my son and it went the full gamut from "Okay" to "All right." My daughter's first book report was longer then the book. It had sentences like, "The girl walked to the door. She put her hand on the door knob. The girl turned the door knob." My son's had the title and the author and, "It was a good book." When my son started high school, someone asked how my son liked it. My husband whispered, "It's a secret."

I give details. If my husband asks me about my day at dinner, he tends to nod off. I usually have to wake him to finish. After all, I want him to know how the day ended and he did ask. On the other hand, when he tells a story, it is pathetic. No details! I have to interrupt numerous times just to find out the name of the person he is talking about. It has gotten so he begins any and all conversation with, "This is all I know about it." What fun is that! I say why bother to talk if you're not going to give details. And gossip, heaven forbid! It goes something like this, "I heard so and so are having an affair." End of conversation. I mean talk about bringing out the devil in me. Some days I just want to strangle him. Does he really think I don't want names here?! If ever details are appropriate, it's when someone is having an affair for Pete's sake. It's a good thing my husband isn't a gossip columnist or we'd be on the welfare roll. Besides, I want to know who has the energy at our age to have an affair. I personally blame middle-age sex on the invention of Viagra. We can be positive it was a male scientist that came up with that little discovery. My husband says he tried Viagra, but it didn't work. You have to go an hour without making your wife mad. And all those Viagra ads, with the caveat if you have an erection for more than four hours, call the doctor. My husband says if that happens to him, he's calling the newspaper! Did I mention my husband fancies himself the court jester?

After supper the other night, my husband said, "Guess who is getting married?" and told me his friend at work.

I replied, "Great! Who is he marrying?"

"I have no idea," he answered, "but we're invited to the wedding."

"When and where is the wedding?" I logically inquired.

To which he responded, "I have no idea."

Call me crazy, but I think details would have been helpful here. I guess we will just drive around until we find a church with a bride and groom in it.

When my sister lived away, she would write epistles. In one such epistle, she described her new drapes down to the pattern on the fabric, the height of the rods, and the diameter of the nails in the wall. It was great! I had a perfect visual image of her entire redecorating scheme. I guarantee if my brother-in-law had written, I would have a visual image of exactly nothing. It would go something like, "We redecorated. Can't find the channel changer." Men out there just don't get it. You can't visualize without details.

I had yet another example of this gender discrepancy in an email sent from my daughter. It was an offensive political cartoon she had received, which she forwarded to her boyfriend and me. My response was no less than one hundred and eight words. Her boyfriend's reply, "Repulsive."

My son called the other day to tell me he'd met the girl he was going to marry. As you can imagine, I almost had a stroke. "Oh, my gosh!" I shrieked. "Who is she? Where did you meet? What color hair? Who are her parents? What's her I.Q.? Her favorite nail polish? Most importantly is she fertile?"

To which he whispered, "It's a secret!"

New York

I'm going to make a confession right now. I love New York! In fact, I love New Yorkers! Okay, all you Southerners out there, go ahead and gasp. I've said it. Stroll down the streets of New York, and you see purple, red, and orange hair. You observe piercings and tattoos. In front of you is every style of dress and footwear. You will witness every ethnic group and religion. Crossing the street or riding the elevator, you can hear five different languages. If I open my mouth, make that six. And the best part of it all—NO ONE CARES! As long as you mind your own business, New Yorkers are perfectly content to let you. Now I personally believe if you witness a mugging or a murder, you should call 911. But, otherwise, everyone seems pretty oblivious to how people look or what they believe. I just think in my naïve little way, the rest of the world should be more like that. But then, that's just me.

One of my best friends from college days is Isabella. Isabella and I head to New York once a year, since she loves New York as much as I do. Isabella is five feet ten inches tall. I, on the other hand, am descended from a long line of elves. She looks like a model and is the most creative person you have ever met, so, of course, she always has the very latest fashion. I will never be mistaken for a model. I am in a constant flux of trying to look like I belong in New York. But I've finally come to the conclusion that it isn't going to happen. Every year, I pack for my New York outing thinking I have the latest fashion—only to get to New York and find out it went out of style the year before. Last year, I did better. I only missed it by a week. This year the style will probably change while I'm in flight.

One year in SoHo (which I realize is the trendy section of New York) I swear I was the only person who matched. Last year, we were strolling down Madison Avenue and a gentleman stopped and asked me directions to Barneys Department Store. I turned to Isabella with this triumphant smile and cackled, "He thought I was from New York!"

"Yeah, right," she replied smugly. "I'm sure the Barney's shopping bag on your arm had nothing to do with it."

Last time I was in New York with my daughter, we stumbled on a movie being filmed with Uma Thurman and Luke Wilson. Of course, we hung around like groupies, trying to get a glimpse of Uma and Luke. It was a street scene with extras, so I suggested to my daughter we lurk in the background and try to sneak into the scene. There is one problem she pointed out. You stand out like a neon light. Everyone (and I mean everyone) had on black and I had on avocado green. My one chance to be in the movies and I, of course, have on the wrong color. It was the year I realized New Yorkers wear black, black, and black.

I was lamenting my faux pas to Isabella. "You know," she pointed out, "you do realize it really doesn't matter. Even if you got the attire right, once you opened your mouth, everyone would know you weren't from New York." Isabella's right, of course. I may as well go back to my tropical colors. Either that or wear black and keep my mouth shut. And I don't have to tell you what my husband said about that.

Ivana Trump And Asparagus

I sabella and I were in New York on our yearly sojourn. We were getting dressed to go strolling in the high end district of Madison Avenue. Madison Avenue is indeed a shopping mecca. Only problem is we can't afford anything. This particular year, Isabella, who is also our travel guide, had emailed me a detailed itinerary of each day's activities down to the exact times. I thought it so clever and had left a copy with my husband. The past two days we had quite successful shopping expeditions and had taken a breather to have lunch at Mercer Kitchen in SoHo, exactly on schedule according to Isabella's itinerary. As we were chatting, the waitress walked up, asked my name, and informed me I had a phone call. Pure terror struck my heart! Something terrible had happened to one of the children. On the other end of the line my husband said, "Has your credit card been stolen?"

"No, I just used it five minutes ago."

"Apparently, the fraud department just called and there has been suspicious and unusual activity on your card."

"Well, I have it right here. I am afraid I am the suspicious and unusual activity."

"I was just hoping it had been stolen," he opined.

That was the year my husband, who has been known to repeat jokes ad nauseam, started this one: "My wife's credit card was stolen. But I didn't report it. The person who stole it was charging less than her." Not long after, my husband was in the hospital for some minor surgery. He tuned into our church service on TV and the preacher used that joke in his sermon. I said, "Are you happy now? You've told that joke so often the preacher's even using it."

But getting back to New York and Madison Avenue, as I have mentioned, Isabella is the fashion maven. I looked down at her feet and she had on these new pointed-toe heels that were all the rage. I said, "Isabella, you're going to walk fifty blocks in those!"

"Aren't they cute? They're Kate Spade and I had to have them. They're fine. I walked around the house in them."

I gave her a very skeptical look but realized it was fruitless to argue. I knew that hell-bent-and-determined look when I saw it. Well, off we go and you guessed it. Thirty blocks up Madison she's lame with blisters the size of silver dollars. It was about this time Isabella realized three hundred square feet of living room is not equal to thirty New York City blocks. The very large blisters on her feet were telling her this little fact. She was in such agony I just couldn't say I told you so, as much as I wanted to. Right then we happened on a consignment shop on Madison. Who knew Madison Avenue had consignment shops? Turns out it wasn't your ordinary, run-of-the-mill one. It was a designer consignment store. There were designer dresses with the price tags still hanging. Did you know some New Yorkers have so much money they buy designer dresses and never wear them? You could buy a $2000 Valentino dress for $1000. How lucky for us peasants on the lower end of the economic rung, don't you think? The shoe gods must have been smiling on Isabella that day because she found a comfortable pair of Pradas for one hundred dollars, never worn of course. She was quite pleased with herself.

Sticking to the itinerary, we headed to lunch at this fancy restaurant on Madison Avenue Isabella had read about in one of her gourmet magazines. Who should we be dining with but Ivana Trump. Ivana, of course, did not realize she was dining with us. She was in the corner with some young thing. If I looked like Ivana Trump, I'd be in the corner with some young thing too. Since Isabella had us eating as much as shopping, I decided to go light and ordered the asparagus appetizer. I do adore asparagus! I knew the price was a little steep but this was Madison Avenue. The waiter brought out six asparagus. "What," I hissed to Isabella, "there's an asparagus shortage this year. This dish cost eighteen dollars. That's three dollars an asparagus!" She, on the other hand, was cackling. The night before, we had gone to the Plaza Oyster Bar. Now Isabella absolutely loves oysters. She had ordered six oysters and paid three dollars a piece. I, being from Florida, regularly get a dozen oysters for three dollars. I could not wait to call my husband and tell him Isabella paid three dollars for one oyster. She was not amused! But she was amused now. "I'm calling your local paper and telling them you paid three dollars for a single spear of asparagus."

When I ventured to the ladies room they had the most wonderful paper hand towels. They would be great for my next luncheon. So I stuck a couple in my purse. I made Isabella go to the ladies room a few times and I went a few more times until I had a set. Like I told her, serves them right. The asparagus was highway robbery. You noticed I never mentioned the name of this particular restaurant. My daddy didn't raise no fool! I have no intention of going to jail for pilfering paper hand towels from the ladies room.

Speaking of the Plaza Oyster Bar, I'm not a big fish eater but I love tuna. I order tuna every chance I get in a really nice restaurant because they always have the best grade. I cannot begin to tell you how wonderful the tuna was at the Plaza Oyster Bar. It was delectable! One bite and I closed my eyes and practically swooned. Isabella said, "Has your husband ever seen that look on your face?"

"Not in a very long time," I answered.

A few months later, Isabella and her husband took a jaunt to Paris. He loves to email and emailed me a detailed description of a fabulous meal they had just enjoyed. I emailed back—get Isabella to tell you about my tuna at the Plaza. He replied, "I already heard about your tunagasm!"

Breaking And Entering

The last time that Isabella and I were in New York, we had quite the drama. We had just gotten out of a cab and reached our hotel elevator when Isabella started shrieking, "I left my wallet in the cab!" Now you have to understand something. Isabella had one of those new, large slouch purses and she had been searching for items in it the entire trip. I naturally assumed her wallet was at the bottom of her purse where it had been all day. Wrong! She really had left it in the cab. Being the friendly Southern girls we are, we pretty much knew all the hotel staff by this point. They went out of their way attempting to peruse the video cameras for a medallion number but to no avail. We learned something new. There are 13,087 taxi cabs in New York City and they are all independently owned. There is no central number so we were directed to the New York Police Department. Like I told Isabella, she had given me a tour of every tourist site in New York, but this was a new one. The NYPD was pretty much like you would expect and I must say the officers were very accommodating. Being the supreme optimist, I kept telling Isabella, once the cab driver found her wallet, he would return it. I was just sure of it. She kept looking at me like I had three heads. While she was filling out the requisite paperwork, a nicely dressed gentleman walked in. It seems he had lost his car. "Kind of puts it in perspective doesn't it," Isabella mused.

As we walked back to the hotel, I'm really proud of Isabella because I am thinking how well she's handling this drama. Then it hits her. "Oh, my gosh! My ID is in my wallet. I can't fly home. They won't let anyone on an airplane without an ID unless you're a terrorist and I'm not a terrorist!" she wailed. As luck would have it, her husband was in Colorado for the week. So we dashed back to the hotel to call her eighty-eight-year-old mother. Isabella tells her mother she is going to have to go to her house, break into it, get her passport, and overnight it. Her mother yells back, "I have lived eighty-eight years without breaking and entering and I am not about to begin now. I don't care whose house it is." Let's just say Isabella inherited her tendency for drama honestly. Well, the conversation went rapidly downhill from that point. Isabella ended up calling a good friend who went to her house, broke in, got the passport, and mailed it overnight.

Of course, I am all the while telling Isabella I am just sure the nice cab driver will drive up to our hotel and return her wallet. She is not amused. We go to the drug store to buy her a surrogate wallet and Isabella, never one to pass up sympathy, described the whole woeful tale to the check out girl. To which the bemused check out girl says, "You left your wallet in a cab. You ain't ever gonna see that wallet again!" Isabella turns to me with an I-told-you-so look. The passport comes the next day. Isabella is once again normal (a relative term I can assure you) and after that drama, the rest of our trip is fairly uneventful.

Two weeks later, the phone rings. Isabella is screaming, "You won't believe it! You just won't believe it! My wallet came in the mail today. The cab driver sent it and every credit card, ID, and money down to the last cent is in it."

I said it three times, "I told you so. I told you so. I told you so." My faith in humanity had been restored. Well, Isabella had made a bargain with God that if she got her money back she would give it all away because she didn't really have the money anyway. Sometimes Isabella's logic is a little difficult to follow. Anyway, she sent half back to the cab driver for being so honest, and gave the rest to the homeless and orphans. Like she said, a bargain is a bargain. And for Isabella a bargain is a bargain, whether it is for shoes or with God.

Mint Juleps

Isabella called the other day in a pure swivet. Seems as though her eldest son was bringing his girlfriend home for the first time and she kept exclaiming, "You're just not going to believe it!" Now, Isabella is known to have an overactive imagination, so I start thinking of all the bad things it could be. The girl's father is a drug dealer doing time? The mother was just committed to an insane asylum? The girl is barren, as in can't produce grandchildren? Isabella had told me this girl was from Long Island, which as far as Southerners are concerned, is as far north as you can get. "You're just not going to believe it," she reiterated for the umpteenth time. "She's never seen *Gone with the Wind*!"

Now there's something you need to understand here. Isabella is *Gone with the Wind*. She is Scarlett O'Hara with the turnip in her hand, who will do anything to keep from going hungry again. Her most treasured possession is a handwritten letter from Vivian Leigh. The mere thought that her son's girlfriend had never seen *Gone with the Wind* was enough to send her to her bed.

But true to form, Isabella had a plan. She and her husband were meeting the unsuspecting couple at the door with mint juleps and fans! I gently suggested they might want to hold off on the antebellum dress and Confederate uniform until they got to know her just a wee bit better. It's a miracle they didn't rent an antebellum home for the occasion. Turns out Isabella's son and this girl did marry and she's not barren. They have a precious little boy, whom they did not name Ashley, much to Isabella's chagrin. They live in Chattanooga, Tennessee, and last I heard the daughter-in-law's mother had moved down the street. I guess the mint juleps took.

Obsession

I called my fashion expert, Isabella, in a dilemma. "I don't know what I am going to do," I wailed. I had just visited my daughter in New York and we had, of course, hit the streets shopping. We found the perfect holiday dress. Finding the perfect dress was not enough. Oh, no! Then I began to obsess. Now I told my daughter, we need the perfect shoes, purse, necklace, earrings, wrap, lingerie, and makeup. "Don't worry," she said most nonchalantly, "I'll find everything."

"Isabella, please tell me. Where did I go wrong? She actually said the words, don't worry." Isabella and I know from years of experience, you don't just worry about fashion decisions, you obsess. After all, any good Southern girl knows accessories make the outfit. Visualize a sequin prom gown with Nikes or the perfect chiffon dress with an ugly black coat. Imagine if you will, a cute cocktail number with flip flops or my personal favorite fashion *faux pas*, bra straps showing. I don't care if it is the fad, it is just plain tacky.

"What am I going to do?" I moaned.

"Well," Isabella replied, "you have several options here. You could send your daughter that magazine that captures pictures of people on the street and publishes them under a big fashion DON'T. If you can imagine the humiliation! Attach a small note asking just how horrible that would be for the world to know she made a fashion *faux pas.*"

"I don't know," I answered. "As blasé as she seems about it all, she'll probably be thrilled to be in a magazine."

"You could just pick the accessories out for her yourself," Isabella continued.

"Well, Isabella, my daughter is an adult and it has been a while since she has willingly let her mother pick out her clothes."

"Okay, you could do what mothers have done for years," Isabella offered.

"Which is?"

"Let her not worry her pretty little head about it one teeny bit and you obsess for her."

"Isabella, you are a genius! I knew you would have the answer."

Let the obsession begin!

Southern Do's And Don'ts

I realize this doesn't interest anyone but a Southern woman from the Old South, but in our region, entire books have been written on the proper place for a lady to put her purse when dining. The problem is there is no consensus. I tried putting my purse in my chair and I sat on it. I laid it on the floor by my feet and the waiter tripped over it. I put it on the table and the salad dressing ruined it. I placed my purse in my lap, forgot about it, walked to the ladies room, and am still trying to find it. I probably flushed it down the toilet.

While in New York, I hung my purse on the back of my chair. The waiter chided, "Madam, why don't you just put a sign on your purse that says 'steal me.' " So sorry, I'm from the South. There they steal your purse, charge on your credit card, return it, and pay you back. If they're really feeling guilty, they pay the late fee. We Southerners are nothing if not polite.

I finally found a purse so small it could easily sit on the table and be out of the way. Only problem, you couldn't get a tube of lipstick in it. But it was really cute and as I've already told you, Isabella says cute is all that matters. So I took it with one-half of a tissue inside.

All Southern women also know the importance of wearing a cute pair of shoes. The last time I was in New York I bought the cutest Kate Spade heels you have ever laid your eyes on. It's true they may have been a wee bit uncomfortable but they were cute, really cute. I wore them to a wedding the other evening. One of our grand Southern dames took one look at my feet and famously exclaimed, "Like I always say. You don't look good if you don't hurt somewhere!"

At that same wedding, one well-endowed young girl had on a dress with quite the décolletage. She was obviously very impressed with her endowment, but frankly she should have known better. Another delightful, elderly dame called me over and loudly whispered, "Just look at those bosoms!" I will have to admit, those bosoms were an eyeful!

You probably won't be surprised to know that in the South whole books have also been written on wearing white after Labor Day. For you non-Southerners out there, this is a big NO—wrong, wrong, wrong! Never mind, we have one hundred percent humidity and ninety degree weather practically year round. It just isn't done. While I am speaking about things that just aren't done in the South, I still remember the first time I saw someone wear white to a wedding and a funeral. In the same week I saw this. Talk about shocked. In the Old South, you never wore white to a wedding. You don't want to upstage the bride. And wear white to a funeral? You may as well announce to the world you're glad to see them go.

It's the day after Labor Day and we're sweltering in the South in ninety degree weather, with global warming and all. I am dressed in black for a wedding with my bosoms covered, wearing my Kate Spade heels, and carrying my microscopic purse. For the record, there's not a dab of white showing anywhere.

Kappa Deltas

The Greek sorority system is alive and well in the South for any of you out there who have been living under a rock. I'm not about to get into a discussion of the Greek system. I just know my most loyal, drop-everything-and-come-running, best friends in the world are Kappa Delta sisters. They are true sisters in everything but blood.

Every fall, nine of us Kappa Deltas meet at the beach house of one of these sisters, who we affectionately call Hon. From the minute we step on the threshold of that wooden porch, we shed all semblances of maturity, responsibility, and sanity. For three days, we are carefree college coeds again, all a size two, with our biggest worry getting a date for the weekend party. It's even better now because we all have husbands and ex-husbands and could care less about getting a date. We just want to party. Add a fair amount of wine and you've got a recipe for one crazy weekend. After looking at some of our rather candid photos this past year, I assured my husband we did straighten up to go to church on Sunday morning. Come on people, we live in the Bible Belt for Pete's sake. We always go to church.

Hon hails from Loo-verne, Alabama (pronounced Luverne in the North). She finds things in'-ter'-rest'-ting.' I know most people pronounce that word in about two seconds with eleven letters and four short syllables stressing the first syllable. Hon, on the other hand, says it with thirteen letters and four long syllables stressing every syllable, all of which takes about thirty seconds. Last time a group of us went to lunch together, she took a gander over at the next table and inquired, "What ya'll havin'? It looks so in'-ter'-rest'-ting." I might add this was not said softly, witnessed by the entire restaurant turning to look.

Hon loves to play games, so following her lead, we had a progressive dinner and went to several restaurants one beautiful sunset evening. Of course, that entailed wine with every progression. I'm not even going to tell you how many new friends we made before that night was over. While looking at the pictures, my husband wanted to know who all those strange people were. I'll be darned if I know. But we were obviously a hit! I remember we talked one guy into proposing to his date and I believe this was their first outing. I doubt if that marriage lasted.

Two of these KDs went with their husbands and grown children to New York recently and took my daughter and her boyfriend out to dinner. From what I have gathered, it turned into a rather entertaining adventure. My daughter called late that evening and the only comment she could utter when I answered the phone was, "Mother!"

"I know. It's amazing any of you children are normal, isn't it?" I opined.

But the truth is we have raised eighteen really amazing children. Allow me to brag for one brief moment here. Among our offspring, we have produced two doctors, two dentists, a CPA, a pharmacist, an English professor, an U.S. Senator's aide, a businessman, a social worker, an education director, a banker, a registered nurse, a property appraiser, and an airline pilot. As one of these KD mothers quipped while we were discussing our children after one especially zany weekend, "It's encouraging to know crazy people can raise normal children!"

We have been there for each other through illnesses, deaths, and some real tragedies. We've been there for the good times too—the births, graduations, weddings, and, one day, we're counting on grandchildren. In actuality, we've closed down one or two weddings. It turns out we were more entertaining than the entertainment—and we were free. Our children have been known to leave their friends and come play with us! So whatever else the Greek system has done, it has given us some of our most fun, cherished moments and true sisters in every meaning of the word.

Beauty Pageants

I don't know what it is about Southerners and beauty pageants, but we love them. Maybe it's the strong scent from all those magnolias that makes us a little crazy. We've got beauty pageants for anyone from one-week-old to one-hundred-years-old. A picture in our local paper displayed the crowned winners for: Baby Queen, Baby King, Tiny Queen, Tiny King, Little Queen, Little King, Pee Wee, Little Miss, Pre Teen, Teen Miss, Best Attire, Most Photogenic, Prettiest Eyes, Prettiest Hair, Prettiest Smile, and Best Personality. I promise I did not make any of the above up. It was a bevy of beauties in diapers. Notice we are not sexist here as we have categories for both sexes. Wouldn't you just love to be a judge for Best Personality for six-week-old babies? For best attire, picture yards of tulle on a two-year-old. And thinking about Best Smile, do six-week-old babies even have teeth? With all those categories, your child could be a winner every few months.

My only foray into beauty pageants was the Junior Miss Pageant my senior year in high school. It wasn't technically a beauty pageant because you were supposed to have brains. That year a group of teachers chose who was going to be in this particular pageant. The bad news was you had to have a talent. That was especially bad news for me. You'll never guess what I came up with? No, I did not twirl a baton. I cannot walk and chew gum at the same time, so I certainly can't throw a metal stick in the air and catch it again while marching with that ridiculous hat on and short shorts riding up my fanny. No way!

I sewed! You heard me right. Amazing, isn't it? Can you imagine if you gave a needle and thread to a sixteen-year-old today. They wouldn't know whether to smoke it or snort it. Talk about an anachronism! Too bad we didn't have videos in those days. My kids would have yukked that one up.

I want to point out I wasn't the only one without any talent. One girl did a dramatic reading. You're thinking Shakespeare, right? No, it was something about a bear hunt! I think she was going for comedy. Another contestant played an instrument. It was not something classical like a violin or cello, but a fiddle! The girl did sit on a bale of hay, so she was at least in character.

One girl actually had a talent, singing. Unfortunately, she got laryngitis and a squeaky sound is all that came out. But she did win Miss Congeniality. It crossed my mind it was a little ironic that the girl who won Miss Congeniality couldn't talk. Maybe that says something about Southern beauty pageants. Suffice it to say, none of us walked away with the Junior Miss crown that year. But there's still hope. We can always pull for our six-month-old babies.

Possum Queen

Speaking of beauty pageants, the only crown I ever managed to snag was in my senior year of high school, Miss Whirlwind. Don't ask! When I went off to college, that being the only title I had ever possessed, I proudly listed it on my recommendation for sorority rush. Isabella later confided to me the sisters got a big laugh off that one. She said that during rush they half expected to see a whirling dervish come spinning through the door. Being the sweet Southern gals they are, they let me in the sorority anyway, bless their pea-pickin' hearts. My children still fall into gales of laughter whenever they see that title next to my name in my high school yearbook. But at least it wasn't Possum Queen. I know what you're thinking, but I'm not making this up. In the little town of Wausau, in the Florida Panhandle, they crown a Possum Queen every year complete with a Possum Festival. They even eat the stuff.

This brings me to an incident that happened a few years after I got married. My husband had given me a mink jacket for our anniversary. Today I wouldn't dream of wearing mink, what with PETA throwing paint on you and all. But back then I admit I was more than a little proud of that mink jacket. One cold Sunday (that would be below ninety degrees in the South) I strutted into Sunday School in my new coat. I was practically preening I am sure. There was a very nice, young couple who had recently joined our class. The young man was a friendly, gregarious sort, quite tall and husky as my grandmother would say. After conversing with him, it was obvious he had been raised and bred in the woods—way back in the woods. Leaving Sunday School that morning, he yelled to me in his robust voice, "That shor is a purty coat. Is it possum?" Now I know what you're thinking. He was joking, right? Well, you're wrong. He was dead serious. With a very red face, I muttered something about not being sure exactly what animal it was. Poor mink, I bet he's the only mink in the universe that's been mistaken for a possum. But I stand my ground. At least I was never Possum Queen.

Nurse Ratched

Best I can ascertain, we Southerners are not a defensive lot. We love to laugh at ourselves. It probably comes from losing the Civil War. My friend Monica is living testimony to this fact.

Seems Monica was helping her best friend decorate for a school Christmas party. Her friend being pregnant, Monica offered to get up on a fifteen foot ladder to put up some lights. Next thing she remembers, she's fallen fifteen feet, flat on her back, on the gymnasium floor. The paramedics come and she is in the ambulance before she becomes fully aware. Thinking she has a broken hip, the paramedic is pulling down her jeans when it hits Monica. She doesn't have on any underwear. Now Monica and I have had this discussion before when I found out the little fact of her not wearing underwear. Like I told her, "What are you thinking, not wearing panties?" I mean the first thing Southern mothers teach their female offspring, as soon as they are potty-trained, is to always wear clean underwear. You just never know when you're going to be in an accident. I told her she was living dangerously here. As the paramedic is pulling down her jeans, Monica moans, "This is one of those times I wish I had listened to my mother. I don't have any drawers on."

"Honey," he replied, "I've seen everything in this line of work." I imagine he has a point there.

They get to the hospital and that is where Monica encounters Nurse Ratched. Barely acknowledging her, Nurse Ratched throws Monica, who by this time is in one of those open air hospital gowns we all love, on an ice cold gurney. As Monica tells it, all she could think about was her "fanny" on that gurney which was most likely covered with all those "superbugs" floating around emergency rooms these days. Monica has a way with words, don't you think? Now she has one arm that is banged up pretty badly from the fall, so, of course, Nurse Ratched grabs that one arm and slings it over the gurney rail for the IV. Monica said obviously Nurse Ratched was absent from class the day they taught how to put in IVs. As Monica is screaming in pain, her best friend, who has accompanied her to the hospital, is telling the nurse, "Don't give her any Demerol."

"Yes," Monica is yelling, "give me some Demerol!"

"No," hissed her friend, "the last time you got that stuff you spilled the beans on everything illegal we've ever done. I have children now. I can't do time."

Soon the technician comes to take her down to X-ray. "But I have to pee," Monica moans. (Sorry, but I have to do the story justice). Nurse Ratched grabs a bed pan, thrusts it under her "fanny," and roughly says, "You can go while he's rolling you down the hall."

At this point, most women I know would have dissolved into tears. I mean Nurse Ratched would have taken the steel out of this magnolia. But Monica's alias is Scarlett O'Hara. She looks Nurse Ratched straight in the eyes and said, "Are you always this mean or just to me because I don't have insurance?"

The technician is rolling Monica down the hospital hall while she's trying to "go," surrounded by a cast of thousands. She asked me, "Have you ever tried to pee in public?"

"Not on purpose," I answered.

"Well, I'm here to tell you, it's a real challenge," she said with emphasis.

Still livid about Nurse Ratched, sarcastically Monica asked the technician, "Does she always have that much personality?"

"I don't know," he answered, "but a broken hip sure hasn't hurt yours."

Turns out there were no broken bones, just some very bad bruises and a slight concussion. As a Southern woman, I'm plum proud of Monica. She stood up to Nurse Ratched and, personally, I think Jack Nicholson is smiling.

New Neighbors

I am not a pack rat. I throw everything away, especially things I need. My husband says in this house you better read the newspaper by nightfall or whoosh, it's out of your hands into the trash. The other day, I threw away a receipt I needed so I was out by the street digging through the garbage can. We had new neighbors and they rode by at that very moment. Not knowing what else to do, I just smiled and waved, like digging through garbage cans was standard protocol in this neighborhood. About a week later, my sister called and needed our family's Christmas menu. Naturally, I had thrown it away so I go outside digging through the garbage can. Of course, our new neighbors drive by. This time they stop, roll down the car window and I quickly said, "If my husband would give me some money, I wouldn't have to do this."

It wasn't long before I had a regular repartee going with my new Southern neighbors. At the end of a Christmas party at our house one year, these new neighbors and another couple were the last to leave. As they all got ready to go out the door, my neighbor quipped to this couple, "Are you my designated walker?"

The wife is a master gardener, who has her yard on home garden tours. She decided it would be fun to open up a little plant shop, and she even threw in a few vegetables for good measure.

I was having trouble with dollar weeds in my grass so I went to her plant stand. She gave me advice which I followed to a tee. It worked beautifully. It killed every single dollar weed, as well as every blade of grass. As we stood gazing at my brown lawn, I said to my neighbor's husband, "I have a great way for ya'll to make your first million. You can get your wife to give advice on killing dollar weeds and then sell sod in her plant stand." Like I said, they have a wonderful sense of humor if you find brown grass funny.

My neighbor finally decided the hassle of a business far outweighed the fun, so she closed shop and marked all her plants seventy-five percent off. It had been a harrowing day quibbling with customers over prices that were already seventy-five percent reduced. She got down to two tomatoes. Two little old ladies walked up to her stand and wanted to know the price of those tomatoes. She said twenty-five cents and one of them sniffed and said that was too high. As my neighbor tells it, at this point she lost it. She grabbed those tomatoes, hugged them to her bosoms, and shrieked, "They're twenty-five cents and not a cent less!" Those two little old women turned and shuffled off muttering under their breath about the crazy plant lady. She said it took all her power of restraint not to bean those octogenarians with her last tomatoes.

As par for the course, I had thrown away something I needed. I think it was quite important like directions on how to get home (See Chapter on Directionally Challenged.) I'm digging through the garbage can by the road and you guessed it. Up drives my neighbor. By this point, he has risen in the world and is now a County Commissioner. He rolls down his window and chirps, "Hi! Thought you might be interested. There's an opening in the garbage collection department. I could give you a stellar recommendation." Next party, he can walk his own sorry self home.

Worry

When it comes to my children, I swear I worry about the craziest things. I would love to know if it is all mothers or just Southern ones. Far be it for me to lie awake at night and worry about the big things, like my children's marriage partners or their careers.

Oh, no! I worry about really important things. Let's say my son has dinner with a girlfriend's parents. Did he use the correct fork? Did he converse with his mouth full of food? Or perhaps my daughter goes out on a date. Did she have bad breath? I've never known her to have bad breath, but there is always a first time! I do believe I could get a call "your son's in jail" and I would think, "Oh, dear! I think he left home without matching socks."

For example, my daughter goes off to college. Do I worry about her eating right or getting enough sleep? No, I worry because I don't think she shaves her legs often enough. One time I sent her a postcard from France. It didn't say "Having a great time. Wish you were here." It just said, "Shave your legs!" Deep down, the main reason I was glad she got a boyfriend, I figured she would shave her legs more often. And you should see her hair brush.

I'm sorry, but it is just not clean enough for me! Like I told her, haven't you ever heard of "cooties?" I know there isn't such a thing, but my daughter doesn't know that, and the odds of her reading a book on entomology are slim to none. Anyway, she would walk in the door from college, her brush in hand, and off I would go to clean it. A little note might come to her in the mail with some sentiment like "Time to clean your brush." She called the other day in a complete panic. Seems without even realizing it, while visiting her boyfriend, she had picked up his brush and started cleaning it! I was euphoric for days.

I even worry about Christmas gifts. My children have to have the exact same number. Just as I get them even, I see some gadget I have to have for my son which entails finding another present for my daughter. Then I see the perfect blouse for my daughter which . . . you get the picture. One Christmas, my son unwrapped a gift of razor blades. I just said, "I had to make it even." Last Christmas, most of his gifts were for his dog but, in my defense, my children had the exact same number of gifts.

You will recall my children have refused to get married. Since my children are single, even though they are practically middle age, I am still counting Christmas gifts. The other day my daughter said, "Mom, don't you think we're finally old enough that we don't have to have the same number of Christmas gifts? I mean we're grown adults here." You may be old enough but I'm not. I had all my shopping done this year when I saw the cutest sweater for my daughter. I just hope my son needs a bar of soap.

Christmas Sweaters

A magazine article caught my eye the other day. A fashion maven was giving five big fashion no's. Number three: ladies, please use all your restraint to keep from wearing one of those Christmas sweaters that have inundated the market of late. If the ladies Christmas coffee I attended the other day is any indication, that little bit of advice never made it past the Mason-Dixon line. Since I have been known to take fashion advice to heart, I swear to you I was the only person there without Christmas apparel. I had on brown. But just for the record, I am not Miss Hildreth and brown is my color. Or at least it is according to Color Me Beautiful.

At this little get-together, there was every shade of red and green sweater known to man. These sweaters were all covered in stockings, Santa Clauses, Christmas trees, ornaments, candy canes, elves, or reindeer. One over-achiever had on all of the above. Add the sequins, glitter, bells, ribbons, buttons, tassel, and all other manner of trim, and you were literally blinded. I had to put on my sunglasses to converse with one lady. One woman had large Christmas trees with blinking lights dangling from her ears. I'm sure she was a lovely individual but I just couldn't get past the blinking trees. I was half expecting her ear lobes to burst into "Oh, Christmas Tree" at any moment. Another lady, and I am not making this up, had on felt reindeer antlers that were lit on the tips. And you should have seen the footwear, red, green, striped laces, pompom balls. It went on and on.

It just happened to be one of those fundraisers where I didn't know that many people, so I can only assume they thought I was an atheist. I'm certainly not giving any fashion advice here but I will tell you one thing. If you're one of those souls having a difficult time getting into the Christmas spirit, I have just the place for you. If that doesn't work, you're a goner!

What Am I Going To Wear?

It is a fact that Southern women spend a disproportionate part of their lives wrestling with the question, what am I going to wear? I mean one of the reasons I don't want to die is I'm afraid the funeral home will get my hair and makeup all wrong. I've already picked out the dress I'm going to be buried in. I mean, Lord, witness Miss Hildreth. The good news is, if it doesn't fit any longer, the undertaker can just leave it unzipped in the back and no one will ever be the wiser.

The only reason I've refrained from killing my husband is I really don't want to wear orange for the rest of my life. Even though on a positive note, that would solve the what-am-I-going-to-wear dilemma. As much as I want my children to get married, those hideous mother-of-the-bride dresses have given me pause. Do you realize there is an entire industry out there trying to make mothers-of-the-bride look, well, motherly? A friend called the other day. She had to go to court with her son for some minor infraction and her biggest concern was what to wear.

Years ago, when I was single, I was obssessing over a party invitation and what, of course, to wear. My very

Southern friend said, "My mother always says, 'Just put on a pretty dress and go. You never know when you are going to meet your intended.'" So I did exactly that. Next morning, I called my friend and said, "Just for the record, my outfit was all wrong. I was completely overdressed. And tell your mother I did not meet my intended. As a matter of fact, if any of the men at that party are my intended, I'm staying single."

My poor daughter, every time she tells me some major event in her life, the first words out of my mouth are, "What are you going to wear?" Deep down I know this is shallow. All those platitudes Southern mothers told their homely daughters like, "It is better to be pretty on the inside," and "Beauty is as Beauty does," are true. You northern girls are probably thinking, what the heck? But us Southern girls were inundated with these pithy sayings our entire childhood. But I just can't seem to help it. My daughter called the other night. It was her first really big job interview. First words out of her mouth were, "Mother, what am I going to wear?" That was music to my ears. I have raised her right!

Colors

I ran into an elderly gentleman friend the other day who was quite perturbed. It seems he had seen a television show called "Queer Eye for the Straight Guy." On this particular show, gay men assisted straight men in dressing stylishly. I'm here to tell you, this gentleman's drawers were in a wad, literally and figuratively, if his dress was any indication. Personally, I'm thinking instead of getting irate, this poor man should have written down some pointers. Now I ask you. What's the problem here? If you've ever been to a cocktail party, you immediately realize ninety percent of the men there need help dressing. Quite frankly, just get help I say!

Talking about fashion, I don't know if this is true in other parts of the country but in the South a color is not just a color. Let me give you a point in fact. I had just returned from a shopping trip in New York after visiting my daughter, who had just spoken by phone with her father. "She said you bought her a yellow dress for the holidays,' he told me as I walked in.

"Canary yellow," I replied. My husband looked at me like yellow was yellow and all Southern women know that just isn't the case.

"She also said you bought two winter coats and they were both gray," he continued.

"One was pearl gray and the other was slate gray," I explained. End of conversation.

A few days later, as I was leaving for the outlet mall, my husband asked me to pick him up some slacks. "What color?" I asked.

"Blue and brown ought to do it," he answered.

"Marine blue, navy blue, dark blue, chocolate brown, mocha brown, latte brown?" I queried.

Through clenched teeth he replied, "I just want blue and brown." Men, why do they always have to complicate things?

We were invited to a Christmas party so my husband asked me to buy him a red tie while I was out shopping. I bit my tongue and didn't even ask one question. I must confess my husband is part of the ten percent of men who do know how to dress. After perusing the tie section in the men's clothing department, I called my husband, and said, "Cranberry red, crimson red, Christmas red, cerise red, blood red, or berry red?

True to form he replied, "I just want a red tie," while stressing each syllable. I had a good mind to buy him one of those ties where Santa Claus pops out and says, "Have you been naughty or nice?" and delete the nice part.

We're getting dressed for the Christmas party and my husband asked if I'm wearing my black dress. "Which black dress? Midnight black, jet black, or barely black?" He just turned and walked out of the room. After we're dressed in our barely black dress and cranberry red tie (I went for subtle this year), I looked down at my husband's feet. "You have on a blue sock and a brown sock," I pointed out.

"I do not," he said.

"Yes, you do. I'm looking at your feet," I insisted.

Looking down he smugly replied, "I have on a marine blue sock and a mocha brown sock."

Names

I realize remembering names is a common malady for numerous people, but my husband defies description. We have to wear name tags in our family, and we're only a total of four. Both our extended families are huge and my husband is clueless. I just advise if someone calls you "uncle" that's a hint they're most likely a niece or nephew. For the record, this has nothing to so with dementia or old age. I realized there might be a slight problem when he got his own name wrong repeating our wedding vows, not to mention by the end of those vows he had married the wrong person.

Early in our marriage when I realized the extent of this problem, I purchased my husband a book entitled *The Memory Book*. The inside flap touted it as a "book that will enable you to remember *anything* the first time you see, read, or hear it." Sounded like a surefire winner to me, so I plucked down $9.95 (this was a long time ago) and presented it to my husband. In a nutshell, it didn't work. One of the book's tricks was to use a catchy term that reminded you of the person. We had an acquaintance, Janice, whose name my husband could never recall, so per the book we came up with "Janice-Wears-Ugly-Jeans." Next time he ran into Janice, he called her Jean. I can only assume one of two things: (1) my husband fudged the truth about actually reading the book, although he is an honest-as-the-day-is-long type, or (2) he didn't remember a word he read. This brings us to the point there is a conundrum in writing a memory book for a person who has no memory.

When my daughter was fourteen, an inexplicable incident occurred that to this day still causes us to alternate between embarrassment and hysteria when we think of it. My daughter had befriended a delightful young man whose name was Kevin. Kevin lived twenty miles away, and since we lived a stone's throw from the high school, he would often be at our home. My daughter and he had several of the same classes so they studied together and he ate supper with us on many occasions. They were in some of the same clubs so they did projects together in our carport. In other words, Kevin was a regular around our house.

My husband had never met Kevin's father and one, now memorable Sunday evening, Kevin had dined with us when his father came to pick him up. My husband went to the front door to meet Kevin's father. Now my husband is a very friendly, never-met-a-stranger type of chap and the first words out of his mouth were, "I am so glad to meet you. We just love Brian." My daughter and I were in the kitchen cleaning up and had just started to go out and greet Kevin's father. She looked at

me with an "oh-no-he-didn't-just-call-him-the wrong-
name" look and started backing away from the kitchen
door. My husband being the outgoing guy he is didn't
stop there. "Really, it has been such a pleasure to get to
know Brian so well. Brian is a delightful young man.
We enjoy talking to Brian so much, and we love having
Brian eat with us." At this point, I joined my daughter
and with every Brian my husband uttered we skulked
further and further back into the kitchen. Poor Kevin!
He was so stunned he couldn't speak, so he and his father
just nodded, said thank you, and made a hasty retreat
before my husband could continue with the misnomer.
Of course, by the fifth Brian my daughter and I were in
hysterics. We couldn't help it but I'll have to confess we
weren't brave enough to go to the rescue. My husband
walked into the kitchen and saw us on the floor in gales
of laughter. "What?" he said.

"Oh, nothing! You just called Kevin Brian five times
enunciating Brian very clearly each time." I can't describe
the look on his face. He was stricken. My husband just
turned and went to bed. He's right. Sometimes there are
just no explanations.

Kevin is now in medical school and my daughter and
he still get a good laugh over the whole incident. Since
Kevin has a mind like a steel trap, he still doesn't get it
but it brings back humorous memories.

My daughter brought her boyfriend home for the first
time recently. Of course, before the weekend was over my

husband called him the wrong name. At least this time, it began with the same letter. Alliteration is a start I guess. My daughter didn't hesitate a second at this juncture. She jumped right in and corrected her father. She wasn't taking any chances this time around. I guess she figured, just in case this young man became a fixture, she didn't want him to go around with the wrong moniker the rest of his life.

Not long after, my husband and I were trying to remember the last name of some neighbors who had moved several years ago. If I can't recall a name for some inexplicable reason I can remember the first letter, so I came up with "C" as the beginning. My husband managed to recall the name had two O's in it. For the good part of an hour, we struggled to retrieve this name from the recesses of our minds. Finally admitting defeat, I called a mutual friend who informed us it was Cook! You would have thought two people working together could have pulled up one small letter from their archaic brains. It's a tad bit scary, but I think my husband is wearing off on me.

I have already cautioned my children, if they should ever deign to get married and have children—in that order, please—they will have to be very careful in naming their offspring if they want any hope of the grandfather actually remembering their offspring's names. It certainly can't be one of those double names so popular in the South like Mary Louise Bowles or John

Parker Sherman. Aristocratic as they are, that would be too much for their grandfather to recall in one sitting. Exotic as they sound, it goes without saying, foreign names are out. Their grandfather can barely speak English as a first language. Anything off the beaten path like Alena or Alessia or Aletha is too much a tongue twister for his particular tongue.

Southerners also have a fondness for calling their sons by their initials, like P.J. or J.P. or G.L., but their grandfather has to have more to go on. I'd probably steer clear of gender neutral names like Kasey or Peyton or Jamie. That would bring the problem of their grandfather remembering whether they were male or female. I wouldn't name sons or daughters after themselves as their grandfather would never know for sure who he was conversing with. Biblical names are definitely out. They have too many syllables. Think about it, Abraham, Absalom, Abednego. Those are definitely too tricky for memory-impaired grandfathers. There are always good old Southern names like Billy Bob or Ella Mae but quite honestly, if I were my children, I would stick with a one syllable name just to be on the safe side. That pretty much narrows it down to Bub or Sue. Surely, with practice their grandfather can remember Bub or Sue.

My husband and I had an argument. Quite frankly, I didn't think he was behaving. My young son came running in to tattle. "Dad called you the wrong name. He called you Bessie Mae."

"Hah! Your father knew exactly what he was doing. Gus and Bessie Mae are your grandparents' first names—his parents," I testily informed my son. I know it's not healthy to use your child as an intermediary in a marital dispute, but frankly I was too miffed to care. I sent the message with my son. "Tell Gus he can fix his own supper tonight."

"We-Know-Mom's-Crazy" Rule

I was reading Dear Abby the other day. A mother was lamenting the fact that her thirteen-year-old daughter would not wear a coat or hat to school in eighteen degree weather. Basically, this mother was pondering if she should put her foot down on this issue or if she (the mother) was crazy. Does anyone else out there see the fallacy in this?

Eighteen degree weather is fourteen degrees BELOW freezing. People get frostbite and hypothermia in that type of weather. Of course, she should wear a coat and hat—a very warm coat and hat. The way I see it, this is how it works. As parents, we make perfectly reasonable requests of our children and they make us out to be the crazy ones!

Allow me to give some personal examples. I may be somewhat neurotic, but I function best in a neat, orderly environment. Call me crazy but I do not like large orange Kool-Aid stains on my beige carpet. I do not care for peanut butter smeared all over the bedspread. I do not want chocolate Oreo crumbs ground into the sofa. The last time I had the sofa cleaned it contained so much food the young man cleaning it ask me if I had ever considered investing in a dining room table. I just smiled sweetly and said I was only the maid. At last count, our house had three perfectly good tables designed for the sole purpose of people eating at them. Is it too much to ask for these tables to be used for that very purpose? Apparently, as my children and my husband call it "we-know-mom's-crazy" rule.

Let me enlighten you with another example. I refused to allow my children to have televisions in their bedrooms. TVs aren't all bad but at best employ passive learning. I guarantee you're not doing any deep, abstract thinking while viewing TV. In fact, most people I observe watching television are comatose, as they don't even appear to have a pulse. We have two TVs in the living areas of our house that can be viewed within limits. But, of course, my children think that is a "we-know-mom's-crazy" rule.

It's gotten so that it is un-American if you don't have a television in every room of your house. I mean even the Post Office and every single doctor's office in the country now have a TV. Just think, by the time I buy stamps, I've learned that people are still fighting each other over religion (of all things), the polar cap has melted another foot, and Britney's been arrested again, this time sans underwear. If this is supposed to make me feel better about paying forty-four cents for a single stamp, let me be the first to inform the Postmaster General, it isn't working.

My kids were in their teens before the advent of cell phones, thank goodness. Have you ever seen anything like the explosion of cell phones? The other day in the mall I saw a new mother strolling her six-month-old baby, who had a pink cell phone in her hand. The mother gleefully said, "She just pushes one when she wants me." Okay, so maybe I made that up. But just you wait, it's coming to that. Anyway, I wouldn't let my children have regular phones in their rooms until high school and then with the caveat they behaved. I was not unreasonable. There was a phone in the den where they could prattle in private. Believe me, the last thing I wanted was to listen to an adolescent's hour-long phone conversation. All those "likes" between every word give me a headache. But again, that wasn't good enough. It was a "we-know-mom's-crazy" rule.

Getting back to my neat gene, I insisted my children take all their assorted possessions out of the car and throw their trash away. Most cars with kids I see look like the local landfill. It appears this out of control penchant for behemoth vehicles in suburban America is just so people have a larger container for their garbage. Call me batty but I do not enjoy riding around in a Dempsey dumpster. But again this was a "we-know-mom's-crazy" rule.

When my daughter was a senior in college, all her best friends were moving into a house off campus and she insisted there was no one else to live with. Frankly, the house was a death trap. On my first tour, I saw electric wires hanging from sockets. The wood was rotting and no telling what manner of varmint was residing under the floorboards. My daughter's bedroom was the windowless attic. In addition, the previous inhabitants had nicknamed this abode "The Brothel." You can imagine my uncontained joy over this little fact. My daughter assured me it was a joke. I saw nothing funny about her residing in a brothel. "That will look really good on your resume," I uttered sarcastically.

Needless to say, I was adamantly opposed to this arrangement. In fact, for a brief moment, I actually wished my daughter was a juvenile delinquent because, quite frankly at this point, I felt jail would be a safer option. She, on the other hand, thought it was a "we-know-mom's-crazy" rule. My daughter didn't see any problem with dangling electrical wires and rat droppings as her decorating scheme.

I will have to confess, I lost this one. She had done too well in college, and I didn't have enough leverage. But I marched right out and bought one of those portable fire escapes. I sat right there until she had read every word of the directions. She kept mumbling she would probably break her leg using it. Let's see, die a fiery death or break a leg. Which will it be? And she is almost a college graduate. But then my daughter put that expensive education to use and pointed out a little fact, that in my frenzy, I had overlooked. There were no windows in her attic/bedroom. So I had to go out and buy an axe so, in case of a fire, she could chop down the wall to use her portable fire escape.

I'm no Dear Abby, but my advice to that mother is stand your ground unless, of course, you want to see your thirteen-year-old lose a hand to frostbite or succumb to hypothermia waiting for the school bus. Let your daughter call you crazy because, quite frankly, by the time she's sixteen you will be.

Party Time

I feel sorry for any parent whose teenager has not thrown a party while they were out of town. It just doesn't seem fair for only some of us to have the joy of raising juvenile delinquents. Besides, it makes for a great topic of conversation. Sometimes I can't help but wonder what the rest of the world talks about. Normally when my husband and I take a trip, I leave my children in the care of a responsible human being. It just seems like the prudent think to do. But this particular trip, I made a serious error in judgment. I left my sixteen-year-old moron with a college student who I sincerely thought was mature. Turns out this college student was a moron, too. According to my son in later accounts, he invited just a few close friends over. Yeah, you believe that. Anyway, regardless of who was actually issued an invitation, the entire junior class showed up. After they filled up the house, they spilled into the yard, the dock, the roadways, and byways.

As this little fete was getting into full swing, seems a group of "thugs" from a neighboring high school showed up. You know the ones. They are of the ilk that make a livelihood intimidating everyone. At this juncture, my neighbor and my son were on the phone simultaneously calling the police. At least my son had the good sense to be a coward. He wasn't about to get his face bashed in. That would hurt. My son had tried football in middle school. He came home whining, "Mom, I got tackled and it hurt!" Who knew football was a contact sport? Anyway, the police came as the thugs fled and emptied my once serene neighborhood of all misbehaving teenagers.

When my husband and I arrived home from our trip, my sister was awaiting us with the glad tidings. Since my bags were still packed, I was sorely tempted to take the next plane to wherever it was headed. Isabella's words from our last New York trip came into my head. As she had so succinctly put it referring to her three sons, "I am more than ready to escape from these people." My husband threw his two cents worth in with: "Look at it this way. Life needs to have some surprises." I didn't even grace that remark with a reply.

You can't count how long my errant offspring was on restriction for that doozy. Not long afterwards, my son ambled into the room where his sister was grousing about some world injustice. "Quit complaining," he said. "I've lowered the bar so low all you have to do is breathe and they're happy."

Soon after, a group of mothers were discussing our sons' latest misadventures. One of the women pointed out a fact. "Remember when we tried to keep our children's little escapades a secret," she commiserated. "Now, I just want sympathy!"

The remnants of the little soiree my son had thrown would not go away. A few days later, as my husband was preparing to fry fish, he poured what he thought was grease in the cooker and it sputtered and spewed everywhere. It turned out it was leftover beer. The same week I discovered a burn spot on the sun porch rug hidden under the sofa. When I pointed this out to my son, he said with dismay, "How did you find that? We hid it so well."

"Well, it would have helped if you hadn't put the rug wrong side up," I ventured. It seems the creative sixteen-year-olds had been shooting firecrackers on the back porch and one misfired and arced back onto the sun porch rug. Honestly, when you think about it, it would be better to leave a room full of two-year-olds unchaperoned than one sixteen-year-old.

Two years later, Jim, my gardener for years, showed up with a beer can. "Found it under an azalea bush by the water," he said. "I don't think I am going to live long enough to find all of them."

My now adult son called the other day to tell me he was going to Atlanta, Georgia, to spend the weekend with friends. "Oh, no, you're not," I replied.

"What are you talking about?" he asked.

"You're not going anywhere. You're grounded."

"Okay," he said exasperatedly. "Please explain this one."

"I was thinking about that party you threw when you were sixteen and we were out of town. You put me through pure agony."

"Mom, that was fifteen years ago. I have mended my ways," he pointed out.

"I don't care. I'm not over it," I snapped as I continued. "I would wish upon you a son who does the same thing but that would be my grandson, so even I know that is not a wise wish. Therefore, I intend on going completely bonkers and embarrassing you at every opportunity that presents itself."

"Well, all I can say," he answered, "is that you're well on your way."

Speed Bumps

I don't know if all cities have speed bumps or just small Southern towns. Is there anything more aggravating, I just ask you? I say if God had wanted us to go slow he wouldn't have given Henry Ford the idea for the automobile.

Our little town has had a mass proliferation of speed bumps of late. I am personal friends with the mayor of our fine city, and love him as I do, I cuss him every time I hit one of those infuriating speed bumps. The other day my son walked in with a knot the size of a baseball on top of his head. "Why didn't somebody tell me they put a speed bump on our road," he grumbled.

"You got off lucky," I replied. "I got a concussion."

I personally think the local body shop is in cahoots with City Hall. They have repaired the bottom of my car so often they gave me one of those hole punch cards. Nine repairs and you get one repair free. I mean, free bagels I can see, but car repairs?

My car has a push button key lock. You push it one time front door opens, two times back door, third time trunk. The problem is my trunk unlocks but I can't tell it. I mean who can count that high? Anyway, half the time I unlock my car only to drive off and see the open trunk light on. I lost count again! The other day I hit a speed bump and you might say I was going a little too fast. Next thing I knew, the trunk flew open, slammed back down, and the trunk light went off. Eureka! I don't have to tell you how ecstatic I was! I finally found a use for those pesky speed bumps.

I was telling my friend the mayor about this amazing discovery. "You know," he said glibly, "I don't know how to break this to you but I don't think that's what speed bumps are intended to do." Really, you don't say?

Churches

One Sunday my family decided to visit a church located on the beach, which is approximately eleven miles from our house. My niece and her husband attend this particular church and when my niece's husband saw us he quipped, "Are ya'll lost? You just passed at least thirty churches to get to this one." He has a point. It is a well-known fact in the South there is a church on every corner as well as a bar and a beauty parlor (that would be a hair salon to you northerners). Come to think of it, I could have had a drink and gotten my hair done on the way.

Churches in the South are part of the environment like azaleas and magnolias. They are more than just religious experiences. They are people's entire social life. Hands down, you won't find better food, and the prayer list alone provides fodder for gossip for a good month. Plus Southern churches can dish out a good dose of guilt. Don't get me wrong. This is not a bad thing. The worse thing I ever did in junior high was pilfer a ten cent tip from a booth in the Woolworth's Five & Ten. I walked around in trepidation the rest of the day and couldn't sleep a wink that night. I ended up sneaking the ten cents back on the booth and praying mightily the same waitress was on duty. It didn't take me long to figure out I should never take up larceny for a career. Not with the guilt factor I carried around.

When my son was five, he snitched a Reese's candy bar from our local drug store. The pharmacist was Mister James, who we all loved. I discovered this theft as soon as we got back to the car, so I marched my young robber right back in that drug store to personally confront Mister James and confess. I'm thinking Mister James is going to put the fear of God in my little thief. Maybe tell him the devil himself will rise from the bowels of Hell and get him if he ever steals again. Unfortunately, I miscalculated Mister James' tender heart, especially when it came to five-year-old little boys. He just patted my son solicitously on the head and said, "It's okay. You can keep the candy bar." All I can say, if my son ends up in the penitentiary for grand theft, it's not because I didn't try.

In our church, when a child turned four they were oust from the nursery into what the kids dubbed "big church" and the parents called purgatory. About a month after my son turned four, the governor of our state came to speak at our Fourth of July service. As you can imagine, we were jammed into the pews. I spent the hour attempting to restrain my very hyper four-year-old from disturbing the folks seated around him. I'm sure the governor's words were very moving, and I'm equally sure I didn't hear a word. The governor ended his message with a resounding

"Amen!" By this time, my son was half on the pew and half under it, clothes all askew. He looked up at me with his big brown eyes and said in a clearly exasperated voice, "That's the longest prayer I ever heard!" At that juncture, all I could do was join in with a hearty "Amen!"

I have to admit one problem I have with my church in the South. They don't think women have enough sense to preach or pray in public. But if the church needs food for a funeral or a wedding or a banquet of two hundred, who do you think they ask to do the cooking? Who do you imagine arranges the gladiolas in the foyer? Who puts together the pageants and stitches all the costumes, banners, and what not? Would you like to gander a guess at who raises all those dollars for the missionaries in China? Why the WMU, of course. That stands for Women's Missionary Union for our northern friends. When's the last time you saw a deacon sewing Joseph's costume or arranging hydrangeas or baking a broccoli puff? Right, exactly never. Let's be frank here. If they didn't serve food at the local church, the place would have to close their doors.

My college alumni magazine came the other day. It highlighted a woman who was a pastor and had become one of the spiritual leaders of her denomination. It was quite uplifting and enlightening. But the entire time I was reading the article, I could only think of one thing. I wonder if her husband can bake a broccoli puff?

The Art Of Bargaining

One of my cardinal rules is never to blow the horn on my car unless it is a matter of life and death. Maybe it's because I am from the South, but I think it is just plain rude. The other day I was very patiently waiting for a parking place at the mall. I say patiently because the lady in the car was putting on lipstick, chatting on her cell phone, fiddling with the radio knobs . . . you know the drill. Just as she finally pulled out, a car dashed right in front of me and got the spot. I'm here to tell you, I broke my cardinal rule. I didn't just blow my horn. I sat on it!

After finally maneuvering into another parking spot, I was going into the mall and ran into a little old lady from my church. She looked me straight in the eye and said sternly, "I saw what happened just now." Why is it you go through life pretty much following all the rules, then the one time you err you get caught? I guess it is kind of how Hugh Grant must have felt. The man is a trillionaire and the one night he doesn't carry any cash, he really could have used a motel room. I was telling my friend what transpired and she said something real intelligent like, "I bet if you had known you were going to run into Miss

Quackenberry, you wouldn't have sat on your horn." You think? On the contrary, I would have rolled down my car window and shouted, "Praise the Lord! I'm so glad you got that parking spot. I was saving it for you." My daddy didn't raise a complete idiot.

In the mall, I passed a swimsuit shop, but at my age I have to take a Valium before I try on swimsuits. Next, I ventured into a new boutique that was way out of my price range. I knew this because in five minutes of scanning price tags, I didn't see anything under one hundred dollars. About that time a very young, voluptuous woman walked out of the dressing room in a very tight, expensive dress. She posed seductively for a very rich, older man seated nearby and purred, "What do you think? Do you like it?"

"It's great,' he replied. "Buy it. In fact, buy whatever you want." Standing there staring at a $395 dress that I most likely would never own, I thought, "I am definitely in the wrong profession."

That same day while I was waiting in line at a check-out counter at a much more reasonably priced store, the lady in front asked me to help her decide which earrings to buy. We had a few minutes discussion on the pros and cons of each, and she selected a pair. Keep in mind, as fellow shoppers, this nice lady and I saw absolutely nothing odd about asking a complete stranger to aid in making a fashion decision. It's a woman thing, I guess. I purchased my outfit and when I got home modeled it for my husband as I was a little unsure of this particular buy. He mumbled, "It's nice."

I questioned, "Nice as it makes my rear end look too big?"

"No," he repeated, "just nice."

Again I asked, "Nice as it makes my bust look too small?"

"I don't know, just nice," he offered.

I'm still unsure. "Nice as it is dull. It doesn't make enough of a statement?"

Rather testily he said, "It's just nice as in nice." With that he goes back to his favorite hobby/sport/exercise, flipping through one hundred and fifty-two channels on the remote control. Obviously, the nuances of fashion escape my husband.

So I do what any sane woman would do. I prance down to the nearest department store and stop a perfect stranger who is female. For five minutes, we discuss the merits of the garment in question. In the end, we decide it is indeed cute but not that cute. I could do better. So I return the outfit and get my money back. If my husband had just cooperated, think of all the time (not to mention gas money) I could have saved. Men can be such illogical creatures sometimes!

Standing in the postal line the other day, I witnessed yet another example of the discrepancy in the different genders' thought processes when it comes to purchases. A young girl had asked to look at the book of the various stamps that could be bought. Being a woman, I imagined she wanted a unique stamp for some special invitation like a wedding or graduation. The male postal clerk was quickly flipping through the pages to show her the selection fully expecting this young girl to make an immediate decision on the stamp of her choice. This young lady politely asked the clerk if she could take the stamp book to a nearby counter to give her more time to peruse the selections. "Ma'am," he replied, "I can't let you do that!" (Did you know postal stamps are top secret information?) This young miss gaped at the postal clerk with a "you-don't-honestly-expect-me-to-make-a-decision-that-quickly" look. The postal clerk, on the other hand, was impatiently staring at her with a "what-is-the-problem-please-make-a-decision" look. After all, to him it was just a stamp for goodness sake. When I left the post office, the poor young girl was standing in the lobby in a befuddled state trying to decide what action to take at this juncture. I submit this as further evidence that as the book says men and women do indeed live on separate planets!

I recall the exact moment my husband realized he might have made a slight error in judgment when it came to bargains and his lifelong mate. We were on our honeymoon in Jamaica. It really was turning into quite a lovely honeymoon, not that I had anything to compare it to, having attempted marriage only once. We were on our way to the straw market, and my new husband had repeatedly cautioned me to bargain. The people expect you to bargain. This had been a constant mantra of his for two days now. Right off I saw this beautiful, handmade basket. "How much?" I asked the nice Jamaican lady doing exactly as my husband had instructed.

"Five dollar," she replied.

"I'll give you seven dollars," I answered triumphantly. My husband whisked me away so quickly it made your head spin, sans basket I might add. Honestly, the lady was really nice and it was a handmade basket. I mean how much time must that take? Isn't that worth anything? It's not like it had been made in China or something. And after all, I was bargaining.

Inner Trouble

One of my college friends and I were emailing the other day catching up on mutual acquaintances. I was inquiring about a friend who had remarried recently. He emailed that the friend was fine but his new wife had inner trouble which was worrisome. Now as we all know by now, I was bred in the Deep South and I am aware of most Southern colloquialisms, but this was a new one on me. I'm thinking what on earth could "inner trouble" mean? So I did what any good Southern woman would do and went to the grapevine for information. None of my other college friends had a clue either and since no one had met the wife in question, we had nothing to go on.

After much conversing, we decided it could be one of several things. Perhaps she had female problems and my friend, who had emailed and is indeed the quintessential Southern gentleman, felt it too indelicate to go into detail. We imagined it could be a religious issue. In the South, it is not uncommon for people to get baptized at an early age, spend their life in the church, and then in adult years began to doubt their salvation. Maybe she had an emotional issue. It could be depression or, I'll admit, we let our minds run a tad bit amok, manic-depression or schizophrenia. Finally, we all agreed it could definitely be a family problem. Perhaps, one of her children was battling an addiction or had gone crazy. The way we see it, the goal is to try not to go crazy yourself before your children do.

Finally, I just couldn't stand the curiosity any longer and emailed my friend to ask him exactly what he meant by "inner trouble." I refrained from that option originally because I didn't want him to think I was nosey. But, quite frankly, I am nosey. Anyway, my friend wrote back, "Oops! Sorry, I had a senior moment. I meant to write inner EAR trouble!" In retrospect, this woman, who we have never met but I am sure is quite delightful, is lucky she just has a case of vertigo. By the time we got through, we had narrowed it down to her child going insane and getting an accidental lobotomy or she herself being an axe murderer. Just goes to show you what a senior moment can do!

Murphy

I apologize to all you animal lovers out there, but I am not one. I don't know why, I'm just not. But it seems like part of being a good mother is letting your kids have pets, so I really did try. We started off with the ubiquitous goldfish that most children have at some juncture. Even this was by default. My sister and I had taken our four-year-olds to the fair and each child had won a goldfish from the carney. My son's was dead within four days after I had invested in the bowl, gravel, seaweed, and coral. My son never did anything halfway. We had to buy out the fish section. My sister, on the other hand, who has been known to be more sensible about these things, bought a bowl, period. My niece's goldfish lived thirteen years in a bowl of water! I kid you not. One time it jumped out and landed on the kitchen floor and another time into the disposal, none the worse. They didn't name it for years because they were sure it was going to die any day. Go figure! This fish was the Methuselah of all goldfish. We win fish from the same carney on the same day from the same bowl and ours dies in four days and my niece's lives thirteen years.

Next we progressed to hamsters. We had four hamsters in all. Princess got breast cancer and we paid $35 for surgery for a $4 dollar hamster. My son looked at me imploringly with his big brown eyes and I just couldn't be a murderer. Hamsters have short life spans so they all died before we could kill them. Even though one winter my older sister did freeze a hamster to death, but if I were her I wouldn't have shared that. I really was burned out on hamsters by the third one, but let my son talk me into yet another. When this hamster died, I didn't say anything. Two months later, my son inquired if anybody had seen his hamster? Needless to say, I had made my point.

Next on the agenda was a cockatiel, which we named Tinkerbell. The truth is the only reason we got a bird is because I loved the cage. It was a wrought iron Victorian number with all those curlicues. It was like my non-athletic friend who took up tennis because she loved all the cute tennis outfits. When I had failed to have Tinkerbell's wings clipped, she escaped from her very beautiful cage. It took us hours to catch her and by the time we did, my house was covered with her "pixie dust." My husband's secretary (who is an animal lover) was the proud owner of a cockatiel by the next day.

Finally my kids laid enough guilt on me until I consented to let them have a dog. Of course they argued for a week about which breed. Finally, I sat them down with an encyclopedia (am I dating myself?) and told them to pick one. They picked a beagle. Since no one in our family knew anything about dogs, my husband went to a friend of his who is an ardent animal lover and the next thing I knew we had a thoroughbred beagle being shipped to us via air from Tennessee. We dubbed him Murphy.

I knew less about dogs than I had about babies, and that was pitifully little. Everyone involved in this process had failed to mention to me they had to tranquilize this poor canine to get him here. As the tranquilizer wore off, you can imagine this dog's state. I have to believe he wasn't a Delta frequent flyer member. In a state of panic, Murphy began racing all over our house going to the bathroom in every corner he could locate. You can pretty much paint a picture of my state of mind by this point. I am thinking what insanity had caused me to allow this dog into my house. Go ahead and commit me, and I'll only make you get one doctor to sign.

In the midst of this whirlwind, the doorbell rang. I answered it to confront a Jehovah's Witness whose first words were, "Did you know the world is coming to an end?" At which point, I emphatically said, "The sooner, the better" as I slammed the door. I didn't have many Jehovah Witnesses visit for a while after that.

My husband arrived home in the midst of this chaos, and realizing I was on the precipice of insanity, he offered to walk Murphy outside. By now the sky was dark and raining cats and dogs (pardon the pun), and my husband was still in his coat and tie from work. He took Murphy to the door, and as he tried to open an umbrella it misfired and made a very loud SWOOSH! Poor Murphy, who was already a bundle of nerves from the events of the day, pulled away from his leash and dashed into the night. We finally found him cowering under a bush.

From that fateful day, when my husband walked out clad for work in coat and tie, Murphy would sit on his haunches and howl as only a beagle can howl. At suppertime, Murphy would start a low, guttural sound which rapidly crescendoed into a keening howl and I would yell, "Kids, your dad's home." My husband saw nothing funny in this. He was constantly muttering about leaving for work with "that dog" howling and coming home to "that dog" howling. Ironically, as long as my husband was in his pajamas Murphy would nuzzle up to him to be petted. I suggested he wear his pajamas to work and change after he got to the office. Quite frankly, he never saw the humor in any of this.

Life with a dog was in'-ter'-rest'-ting'. The first time I attempted to clip Murphy's toenails, I drew blood. That dog grabbed those clippers, ran through the dog door, and buried them in the yard. I'm thinking, "Great, that's all I need. One more smart, stubborn addition to this family." Of course, the novelty of a dog wore off for the children, but he became my third child. Murphy even made our Christmas card every year. Like my kids, he was always one step ahead of me. I never did break Murphy from sitting on the sofa, and believe me, I tried everything from doggie treats to shock therapy. I finally had to concede the truth. Murphy was just plain smarter than I am.

As it turned out for us, it wasn't such a good idea to buy a thoroughbred. It seems all that inbreeding caused a genetic disease. After only four short years, Murphy died suddenly from a heart defect. I was inconsolable and it just about did me in. I have the fondest place in my heart for that neurotic little animal. A little part of me will always miss him.

Not long after Murphy's demise, my husband walked in from work and I started howling. He looked at me like I was an insane woman. "I'm just trying to make you feel at home. I know how much you miss Murphy." He was not amused. Personally, I think he needs to work on his sense of humor.

The Aristocracy

Recently one of my childhood friends confided that growing up she considered me a part of "the Aristocracy." You could have knocked me over with a feather! This was news to me. As far as I was concerned, growing up my family was neither rich nor poor.

In my day in the Deep South, there were three topics that were never discussed in polite company. It goes without saying that first and foremost among the taboo topics was sex. I was aghast the first time I saw the Olympic gymnast, Cathy Rigby, in a television commercial for sanitary products! I seconded the sentiment of the wonderful Southern humorist, Lewis Grizzard, when he said, "I will be so glad when Cathy Rigby goes through menopause."

The second topic never discussed was bodily functions. I vividly remember when I was eight years old and said dog "poop" in front of my sister's boyfriend. If my mother's look could have killed, I would not be here today. It has taken me over fifty years just to write the word and I have yet to utter it aloud again.

The third taboo subject was money. Discussion of money was considered just plain tacky. In addition, my father was known to be quite thrifty. There are two stories that come to mind. When the first McDonald's opened in our little town, every Sunday night I drove my younger sister and brother there to eat. My Daddy handed us one dollar. One dollar could buy three hamburgers, three drinks, and TWO french fries. We put the french fries in the middle seat and fought over them. I am convinced my brother's feistiness was a result of fighting for his french fries!

The one time my father made an exception to his frugal ways was my senior year in high school. I have been a prattler since I was birthed, and every time Daddy called home, the phone line was busy. One day in a fit of irritation over an eternally busy phone signal, my father had a private phone line installed for me. A year later, as I was finishing packing on the day I was to leave for college, I looked up to see a strange man standing in the doorway of my room. "Yes?" I asked very puzzled by his presence.

"I am here to take out your telephone line," he politely answered. You would have thought Daddy could have at least waited until I locked my trunk!

In college, I finally got some insight into the money issue. I realize that in today's world the only criterion for buying a sixteen-year-old a car is that he or she is breathing. I, on the other hand, had to graduate from high school and college (with honors no less) before my father purchased me a very basic car. As I recall, it had no radio or air conditioner. Thus, I had no car in college, which was not a problem until I immediately fell madly in love and my boyfriend and I were separated for the summer. At home, I pleaded with my father to visit Birmingham, Alabama, to see my boyfriend for the weekend. Daddy finally consented to spring for a ticket on the Greyhound bus. I was so in love that I would have ridden a camel, so I jumped at the offer. Birmingham, Alabama, was three hundred miles away—five hours by car. It took twelve hours on the Greyhound bus! Suffice it to say, the bus stopped often and for long periods of time. During one of the stopovers, a boy about my age sat next to me. It was not long before I realized he lived deep in the country—and that he was garrulous and inquisitive. After peppering me with numerous questions about myself, he stated, "So, money is no object for you." It dawned on me, if I was a member of "the Aristocracy," no one had bothered to tell me, because in the Deep South you just did not talk about money.

True to form, at eighteen-years-old my daughter fell madly in love. The young man was at the Naval Academy, and she begged to go for a visit. I did have the good sense not to let her drive a thousand miles to Baltimore, Maryland, because, of course, we had bought her a car when she turned sixteen. After all, she was breathing. So with fond memories, I suggested the Greyhound bus. Being idiotically in love, she jumped at the idea. It took a week to get to Baltimore! Okay, I exaggerated again, but it took a very long time. Then she had to return home. Blinded by love, she had forgotten that little detail. As she pointed out after her return, "I spent longer on the Greyhound bus than I did with my boyfriend."

The thing is that was my plan from the beginning. If you should ever happen to meet my daughter, I would appreciate it if you would refrain from mentioning that little fact to her.

A Southern Belle Errs

I think I have made it abundantly clear, in my day in the Old South, being polite was not an option. My grandmother taught me at an early age that you are always polite and respect your elders, which usually means those in authority. If you didn't like it, too bad, get over it. The world does not revolve around you.

Recently, I was driving through a residential area on my way home. Glancing into my rear view mirror, I saw a police car with flashing lights. "That's odd," I thought puzzled. "I wasn't doing anything wrong."

As I rolled down my car window, a twelve-year-old policeman approached me. Very politely I inquired, "Is there a problem, sir?"

"Yes Ma'am, you were speeding," he replied.

"Sir, I was driving 34 miles per hour," I tersely answered.

"Yes, but this is a 25 mile per hour zone."

Knowing I was headed in the wrong direction, I snipped, "Surely you are not going to give me a ticket for going 34 miles per hour. That's absurd!"

"I don't think driving 9 miles over the speed limit is absurd," he nervously replied. As he asked for my driver's license and car registration, I noticed a slight tremor in his hand. He was beginning to suspect he had stopped the wrong Southern woman. Stewing, I practically slung my license and registration at him.

After a few minutes in the police car, the officer walked back to my window. I really was trying to get a grip here, but it was not working. "Just so you know, I am NOT happy about this," I hissed. Jumping back a bit, he rattled off all the instructions for paying my $125 speeding ticket. "Fine," I snapped as I grabbed the ticket and, in not my finest hour, said something sophomoric like, "Now, go catch a real criminal!" Actually, that is exactly what I said.

He looked at me very seriously and responded, "But Ma'am, I can't. I am only a traffic cop!"

Since my driving record is a bone of contention in our household, I very prudently hide these occasional incidents from my husband. But feeling unjustly wronged and seeing the humor in this, I went straight to my husband's office and relayed the entire episode while he shook his head in dismay throughout my rather dramatic narration. His only response was, "The cop should have gotten you for assault and battery."

Within no time I felt mighty guilty about my behavior. This Southern belle had greatly erred! So I went to the cemetery to talk with my grandmother and took real flowers—not those ersatz plastic things. As I told Mama Byrd, "I know you taught me better. I greatly erred even if the policeman was only twelve-years-old and I really wasn't speeding. I made a mistake in committing only a misdemeanor, because if it had been a felony he couldn't have stopped me, him being just a traffic cop. I've learned my lesson. Next time, I'll go for robbery." I am pretty sure I heard a chuckle when I left.

Fast forward, three weeks later. It had already started off as an aggravatin' morning. You know those days. My car was in the shop, and I had to drive my husband to work so I could use his car. I forgot the clothes for the cleaners, so I had to drive all the way back home to get the darn things. Same location, same speed, same policeman. He even pulled me over in the exact spot. When I saw the identical twelve-year-old policeman approaching, I knew I was in big trouble. Before he could barely get to my car, I rolled down the window and said in rapid English, "Sir, I am so sorry. I know better than to go fast in a residential neighborhood. I was distracted and just not paying attention. I am really sorry. I am making a mental note to myself right now to pay better attention when I'm driving and be more careful."

At that point I had a glimmer of hope as I realized the policeman had not recognized me from our prior little get-together. Somewhat startled after my unexpected litany, he simply said, "May I please see your driver's license and car registration." Knowing the drill, I already had these items in hand. While he was in his police car, I did what any sane person would do when they find themselves in a bind. I promised God everything but my first-born child if he would just get me out of this one. Luckily for my first-born, I wasn't mad at him that day or I would have promised him to God too.

Arriving back at my car, the policeman says, "Ma'am, I see I pulled you over here a few weeks ago. Do you remember that?"

Squinting my eyes as if deep in thought, I replied, "You know, I think it's coming back to me."

To my new friend's credit, he proceeded to explain nicely that the precinct had received complaints from the neighbors about speeding cars. He did not want me to get in the habit of speeding, so please, watch it, and he would just issue me a warning. (Thank you, Jesus!) But, I had given him the wrong car registration. I quickly explained I was driving my husband's car because mine was in the shop. Too bad, he needed the car registration for the car I was driving. After turning the car upside down sans registration, the policeman gave me a ticket to go to the courthouse and produce the correct car registration. This would only cost ten dollars. Driving off, it dawned on me I was probably going to have to do penance for the rest of my life after all my promises to God.

Now I had a new dilemma. There was NO way I could tell my husband I had been stopped a second time for the same offense. However, I had to find his car registration, which was most likely in his wallet. My husband keeps his wallet on the bedside table, so that night when he started snoring, I furtively slipped the registration out of his wallet. I arrived at the courthouse the next morning—only to be told the ticket had not been processed yet and to come back later. That night I stealthily put the registration back in its place and repeated the whole sneaky process a week later. I decided then and there, it is true—crime does not pay!

I knew I would have to confess my sins eventually. A week later, I arrived home and my husband had cut a notice out of the paper. It was alerting residents that the police were patrolling Florida Avenue—the scene of my recent crimes. "I thought you might need a reminder," he said peering over his glasses at me.

"Well, now that you brought it up, I've been meaning to tell you about my latest rendezvous with the law."

After my timorous explanation, he just shook his head and said, "How do you make these errors? Do you remember the lotion?"

It seems a while back, when I was ordering lotion from Avon, I had inadvertently dialed a 900 number instead of their 800 number. I heard a musky, sexy voice saying, "I've been waiting for you to call."

"Wow!" I thought, "Avon is really good. They knew I was going to call."

The sultry voice continued, "I'm getting ready to show you the time of your life."

"Whoa!" I thought, "There's some mistake. I just want lotion." Finally realizing my error, my face beet red, I slammed down the phone.

That evening I told my husband this little incident. He looked at me in amazement and said, "You are the only person I know that can call for lotion and get sex!"

The South

We took our son to Boston on the obligatory trip to learn about the founding of our great country. Other than the fact Bostonians talk funny, I love Boston! How could you not, what with all that energy zinging about.

We almost lost my husband on the first day. An attractive young girl at the front desk was helping my husband and me with sightseeing information. A little side note is in order here for all you non-Southerners. In the South, we address ladies "Ma'am" and it is a sign of respect. I mean growing up in the South if you didn't say "Yes, Ma'am" or "No, Ma'am," you got a spanking sho' 'nuf. Being his polite Southern self, my husband began, "Ma'am," and the young lady quickly interrupted, "Don't call me Ma'am."

Somewhat startled, he said, "I'm sorry, Ma'am. I didn't..."

"I believe I said don't call me Ma'am."

Flustered my husband replied, "Ma'am, I am so sorry..."

"DON'T call me Ma'am!" the young lady said once again, this time with more emphasis.

Now so flustered he is blubbering, "Really, Ma'am, I mean, Ma'am, I didn't mean. . . ."

"I said DON'T CALL ME MA'AM!" This lady's message was very clear by now. At this point, my husband had broken out in a cold sweat. Quickly assessing the situation, I grabbed my husband by the nape and dragged him across the hotel lobby as he yelled, "My apologies, Ma'am.."

Safely ensconced in the elevator, I shook my head in dismay and said, "Please, for the next five days try to remember you're in the North." We considered changing hotels but it seemed too much trouble, so we skulked around the rest of our stay, cautiously avoiding the offended young lady at the front desk.

As we left the hotel headed to Maine, we decided to double check the interstate route since my husband was not up for losing another $100 over directions. We spied a policewoman across the street. I rolled down the car window and in my very best Southern drawl loudly yelled, "Ma'am, could you help us out?"

I know what you're thinking here—slow learners—very slow learners. Well, I'm here to tell you, the entire sidewalk froze, turned, and stared, and this being Boston, that is quite a few people. All I can say is at least I picked a policeperson with a sense of humor. With a grin on her face, she approached our car and said to a very red-faced Southerner, "You're not from here, are you?"

"No Ma'am, I'm not. I'm from a foreign country. It's called the South. You ought to visit sometime. It's a real nice place!"

About The Author

Photo by Ruth Berry

Olivia deBelle Byrd was born and bred in the South. She is a graduate of Birmingham-Southern College and a Kappa Delta. She resides in Panama City, Florida, with her husband, Tommy, and is the proud mother of Tommy Jr. and Elizabeth.

BUY A SHARE OF THE FUTURE IN YOUR COMMUNITY

These certificates make great holiday, graduation and birthday gifts that can be personalized with the recipient's name. The cost of one S.H.A.R.E. or one square foot is $54.17. The personalized certificate is suitable for framing and will state the number of shares purchased and the amount of each share, as well as the recipient's name. The home that you participate in "building" will last for many years and will continue to grow in value.

Here is a sample SHARE certificate:

YES, I WOULD LIKE TO HELP!

I support the work that Habitat for Humanity does and I want to be part of the excitement! As a donor, I will receive periodic updates on your construction activities but, more importantly, I know my gift will help a family in our community realize the dream of homeownership. **I would like to SHARE in your efforts against substandard housing in my community!** *(Please print below)*

PLEASE SEND ME _____ SHARES at $54.17 EACH = $ $_____

In Honor Of: _____

Occasion: (Circle One)   HOLIDAY   BIRTHDAY   ANNIVERSARY

    OTHER: _____

Address of Recipient: _____

Gift From: _____ *Donor Address:* _____

Donor Email: _____

I AM ENCLOSING A CHECK FOR $ $_____ **PAYABLE TO HABITAT FOR HUMANITY OR PLEASE CHARGE MY VISA OR MASTERCARD** *(CIRCLE ONE)*

Card Number _____ Expiration Date: _____

Name as it appears on Credit Card _____ Charge Amount $ _____

Signature _____

Billing Address _____

Telephone # Day _____ Eve _____

PLEASE NOTE: Your contribution is tax-deductible to the fullest extent allowed by law.
Habitat for Humanity • P.O. Box 1443 • Newport News, VA 23601 • 757-596-5553
www.HelpHabitatforHumanity.org

CPSIA information can be obtained at www.ICGtesting.com
Printed in the USA
LVOW07s1913020216

473410LV00001B/1/P